HOW TO
DISSECT

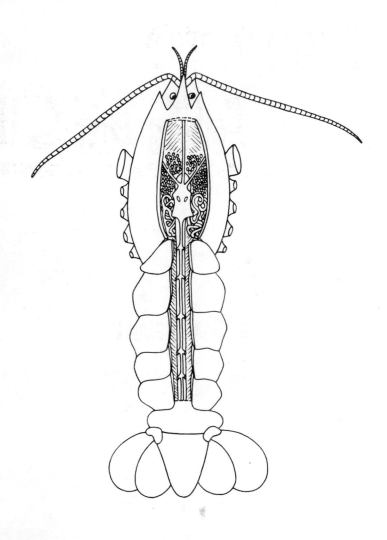

HOW TO
DISSECT
EXPLORING WITH PROBE AND SCALPEL

WILLIAM BERMAN

Chairman (Retired) of the Department of
Biological and Physical Sciences
S. J. Tilden High School
Brooklyn, New York

ARCO PUBLISHING COMPANY, INC.
219 Park Avenue South, New York, N.Y. 10003

Acknowledgment by Author:

To my wife, Betty, whose skillful editorial incisions helped to shape this book and to the publishers whose insatiable "whys" brought the author closer to the reader.

Drawings prepared from author's sketches.

Third Edition, First Printing, 1978

Published by Arco Publishing Company, Inc.
219 Park Avenue South, New York, N.Y. 10003

Copyright © 1961, 1965, 1978 by William Berman

Library of Congress Cataloging in Publication Data

Berman, William.
  How to dissect.

  Includes index.
  1. Dissection.   I. Title.

QL812.B4   1977   591.4'028   77–4716
ISBN 0–668–04325–3 (Library Edition)
ISBN 0–688–04331–8 (Paper Edition)

Printed in the United States of America

CONTENTS

Dissection Is Adventure 1

YOU ARE about to embark on a new kind of adventure. With probe and scalpel you will explore the anatomy of animal and plant life. Dissection not only reveals the architectural plan of living creatures; it also shows how life has evolved from the simple to the most complex forms.

This is not a "cook book" of dissection "recipes." Our directions for dissecting must be, and we hope they are, clear and easy to follow. But you should go beyond the limits of dissection itself. For the inquisitive young scientist with questions which exceed the scope of this book, we have included suggestions for more advanced work. For example, in addition to dissecting the earthworm, you might want to study its ability to solve problems! In addition to dissecting a flower you may want to look into the problem of developing a method of supplying food and oxygen for our travellers in outer space. Dissection is a tool, a technique of investigation used in the service of science.

You will retrace the steps of some of the great biologists. You will travel along roads branching off to other roads, and at the end you may find yourself in new bypaths, yet uncharted by science. In these days of expanding scientific knowledge, young scientists often find themselves advancing toward the frontiers of research. You will meet some of the unsolved problems and stirring challenges facing our scientists. Perhaps some day you will help find the answers to some of these problems.

In your work with dissection you may find the answer to your own future. Do you want to be a doctor, a science instructor, a dentist? Perhaps you would rather be a chemist or a physicist, doing research in cancer, in heredity and in many other vital areas. The choices are many and are often bewildering. Few of us make early decisions. We all need guidance. This book can help give you a start in mastering background you will need before you can determine whether you are suited for a profession in science. Besides promoting a knowledge of anatomy that will increase your understanding of the human body, it can provide evidence of your own aptitudes and capabilities. You may decide to join the dedicated army of scientists and make research your life work.

This book should be especially helpful to biology students from the secondary school through junior college and freshman college levels. It will be useful to students in advanced courses in high school zoology and in advanced college placement biology courses in high school. College students will find that our simplified dissecting techniques and directions will enable them to benefit more thoroughly from their required readings in physiology, evolution and other related topics.

Most people have a strange notion about dissecting. They see themselves standing in a pool of blood, gripping bloodied instruments. This notion is all wrong. A dissection is clean. The only "blood" present in the prepared specimen is the latex injected into the blood vessels in the biological supply house by which the arteries are stained red and the veins blue. This "color map" helps us trace the circulatory systems. When you receive the specimen it has already been treated with preservatives to keep the tissues from hardening and drying out. All you need do before dissecting is to wash away thoroughly the excess preservative under running water.

Another false notion about dissecting is that all you do is cut and slice. A specimen is not a loaf of bread; it is a marvelously assembled and intricate set of structures held together by tissue, mostly connective tissue. You might compare a specimen to a carton of fragile, expensive dishes you are about to open. Each article is separately wrapped and you are going to unwrap it very cautiously. That's what we do when we dissect; we make careful incisions to expose parts. We then use a probe (often called a seeker), a long, thin, pliable metal rod with a smooth, rounded tip, to separate organs from their coverings. In a sense, we are carefully unwrapping the parts of the specimen without injuring any of the parts. Except for major incisions, *don't cut—dissect!*

All you need to profit from this book is the curiosity you were born with, and the ability to read well enough to understand and to follow directions. However, this is not the kind of book that can be merely read as you would read a novel. Except for the introductory remarks in each chapter, you must work with the specimen before you because the text and the illustrations or diagrams refer to the specimen. It often happens that many organs which may be difficult to visualize from the text can readily be seen in the specimen. The diagrams have been simplified to make it easy to identify parts on the specimen. A picture may be worth a thousand words, but the real thing is better than a thousand pictures. To avoid confusion, very small blood vessels and nerves are not shown in the diagrams. After you have mastered the main techniques of dissection you might consult a more advanced book on comparative anatomy for more technical study.

The dissections have been arranged so that we begin with relatively simple, primitive specimens and work our way up to the more advanced forms of life. We begin with the earthworm, a spineless creature, and close with the frog, a vertebrate animal with a well developed spine which, in many structural features, is similar to man. The dissections provide a fascinating glimpse into the story of evolution. The basic techniques for dissecting the earthworm are used in dissecting more complicated specimens. However, each new dissection will require additional skills. When you have dissected the crayfish you will gain the basic training for dissecting the grasshopper. Dissecting the shark is excellent preparation for dissecting the frog and the frog dissection is a fruitful basis for the dissection of a mammal, the fetal pig. The more dissecting you do, the more you will get out of this book.

Important Points for Successful Dissections

Before dissecting, read directions carefully and examine accompanying diagrams thoroughly. When dissecting, turn the dissecting pan to the position most comfortable for you as you handle the instruments. Use the probe often for separating structures (veins, nerves, organs) from connective tissue, and for tracing the course of hollow structures by inserting the probe to see where they lead or originate. Trace and master one system at a time. Then see how the different systems are related to each other and to the general body plan.

Specimen jars.

Dissecting pins.

Dissecting scissors.

Straight-tipped forceps.

Dissecting pan.

Curved-end forceps.

Thin, curved-end probe.

Thin probe.

Dissecting microscope.

Dissecting needle.

Hand lens.

Scalpel (medium size).

Fig. 1. Basic Dissection Equipment.

Dissection is analytical. Separating and analyzing associated parts provides us with the basis for productive thinking when we assemble data to produce new ideas. When you dissect or take apart an organism you are taking the first step toward putting together, or synthesizing, new theories and new knowledge. Do not be satisfied with dissecting only one example of a whole group of animals. Use the knowledge and skills you have gained in independent learning.

At the end of each chapter you will find ideas for exciting research, for science projects and for enjoyable hobbies. Make your own diagrams and keep records of your dissections and findings. Compare the systems of every animal and plant you dissect to discover evolutionary connections. Take photographs of the dissections. Each animal has its own story to tell. No dissection can be adequately meaningful if it is done as a single experience. It is like trying to judge a painting without having examined and analyzed other paintings.

What equipment will you need for dissection, in addition to the specimens? There are certain basic tools that will be useful in all dissections. Individual instruments or fully equipped dissecting kits may be obtained from biological supply houses and hobby shops. Additional instruments with special advantages in particular dissections are described in the text where they are needed. Following is a list of basic equipment:

Dissecting pan	Paper towelling
Dissecting pins	Single-edge razor blade
Dissecting needles	Straight-tipped forceps, medium size
Specimen jars	Curved-tipped forceps
A thin probe	Hand lens, 5x to 10x magnification
Scalpel, medium size	Dissecting microscope, 5x to 10x
Dissecting scissors, 4 to 5 inches long	

Formaldehyde preserves specimens or organs for future study. A good mixture for preserving most specimens is a 4% solution of formalin, which is made by adding 4 ml of commercial formalin to 96 ml of water. The mixture is a very weak solution of formaldehyde. A little cold cream rubbed into your fingers will prevent the preservative from dehydrating your skin.

Transverse plane.

Cephalic (head) region.

Caudal (tail) region.

DORSAL.

ANTERIOR. ———————————— POSTERIOR.

VENTRAL.

The compass points of anatomy (anterior, posterior, dorsal and ventral) appear in all forms of animal life from the simple, spineless creatures to man himself. These compass points help us observe how animal life evolved from a crawling stage to an upright position.

Fig. 2. The Compass Points of Anatomy.

Order double-injected specimens by their scientific names as indicated in the text. Double-injected specimens are injected with two different colors—red for arteries, blue for veins.

Important Technical Terms
And finally, here are a few of the important technical terms frequently used in dissection:

> *Dorsal*—the back or upper part of the animal
>
> *Ventral*—the abdominal side or lower part of the animal
>
> *Cephalic*—the head region
>
> *Cranial*—the upper part of the head
>
> *Anterior*—the forward or front end of the body
>
> *Posterior*—the hind or rear part of the body
>
> *Caudal*—the tail end
>
> *Transverse*—the cross section
>
> *Longitudinal*—along the length of the body.
>
> *Proximal*—nearest to, or at point of origin or attachment
>
> *Distal*—farthest from origin or point of attachment
>
> *Sagittal*—along the median plane

There are many other technical terms used in dissection, but if you understand these terms you are ready to begin.

Did we say begin? Just so!

2 Night Crawlers in the Laboratory

MANY OF us have had the fun and excitement of fishing with an earthworm as bait. But few people realize how important the earthworm is to civilization. This lowly creature is one of Nature's greatest cultivators. Charles Darwin, one of the world's famous scientists, estimated that in England's farmland there were over 50,000 earthworms to the acre. He calculated that these worms turn over 18 tons of soil per acre and bring one inch of rich soil to the surface every 5 years. While this estimate may not be accurate for all tillable areas in the world it shows that our little friend, the earthworm, enriches farmland and helps indirectly to provide more food for a rapidly expanding world population.

Another benefit plants and animals derive from the earthworm is that the soil becomes more porous and air circulates more readily through the earth because of all the burrows or holes made by the earthworm. This helps to support living things in and on the soil.

Night Life of the Earthworm

The earthworm hunts for food at night. That is why it is called "nightcrawler." Its food is fallen leaves and animal debris. It usually extends its body from a small burrow which it creates by literally eating its way through the soil. The hind part of the worm's body remains near the surface end of the burrow while the rest of the animal forages for food. If it is disturbed by its mortal enemy, the robin, who hunts the earthworm during the day, or by any unwelcome nocturnal intruder, it retracts its muscles with remarkable speed and tries to escape into its underground retreat. If the earthworm is undisturbed it will swallow leaves, small particles of earth and other material. This food is acted upon, with the help of the earth it swallows, by the worm's digestive system. In this way the worm gets its nourishment, while its wastes help to fertilize the soil.

Why do we select the earthworm as our first subject for dissection? The earthworm is a lower invertebrate (an animal without a backbone) which has a simplified pattern of structure. A study of the earthworm's anatomy will therefore provide us with a key for unlocking the secrets of structure in higher forms of invertebrate animal life and will also furnish some clues to understanding man's anatomy.

Materials Needed

For our first dissection we will need preserved injected specimens of earthworms, *Lumbricus terrestris*. More than one specimen should be purchased because the first specimen may be damaged through inexperience. An injected specimen is preferable because the structural systems of the worm, particularly the circulatory system, will show up more clearly. We will also require the following equipment:

A dissecting pan.

A quart size bottle of formaldehyde which is to be used as a preservative if the dissection is carried over to another day. (Keep the bottle tightly sealed when not in use to prevent the odor from spreading.)

Two or three small specimen jars with covers, in which to store the specimens. Specimens may be kept almost indefinitely in formaldehyde.

Dissecting pins to pin the specimen to the dissecting pan. Keep a good supply on hand.

A 5x to 10x hand lens to examine small parts of the specimen.

An inexpensive 5x to 10x dissecting microscope.

A pair of fine surgical scissors 4 to 5 inches long with one sharp tip and one blunt, rounded tip for use in cutting through parts of the body.

A medium sized scalpel to cut through skin and tough tissues.

A sharp, single edge razor blade for starting incisions.

A pair of curved-end, fine-tipped forceps for use in holding tissues that are to be dissected or examined.

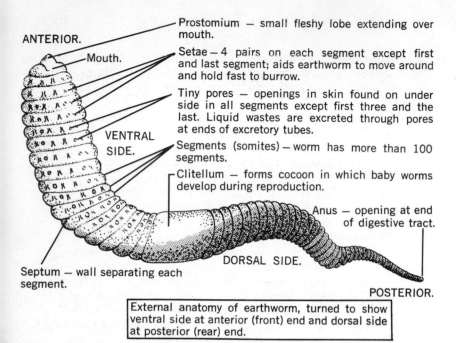

ANTERIOR.

Prostomium — small fleshy lobe extending over mouth.

Mouth.

Setae — 4 pairs on each segment except first and last segment; aids earthworm to move around and hold fast to burrow.

Tiny pores — openings in skin found on under side in all segments except first three and the last. Liquid wastes are excreted through pores at ends of excretory tubes.

VENTRAL SIDE.

Segments (somites) — worm has more than 100 segments.

Clitellum — forms cocoon in which baby worms develop during reproduction.

Anus — opening at end of digestive tract.

DORSAL SIDE.

Septum — wall separating each segment.

POSTERIOR.

External anatomy of earthworm, turned to show ventral side at anterior (front) end and dorsal side at posterior (rear) end.

Fig. 3. External Anatomy of the Earthworm.

A thin probe for exploring body tubes and for separating structures from their membranes.

Dissecting needles for separating organs from their membranes, pinning down dissected parts, etc.

Paper towelling to clean and dry instruments and to dispose of the dissected specimen in a rubbish barrel or incinerator.

External Anatomy of the Earthworm

Before we begin actual dissection we should become familiar with the external anatomy of the earthworm. With Fig. 3 as a guide let us proceed to examine the specimen. Note that the dorsal (upper) side has a darker coloration than the ventral (lower) side. The bristles (*setae*) which enable the earthworm to move about and hold firm to the ground are found only on the ventral (lower) side, as are the tiny pores on the body wall. The earthworm breathes through its moist skin. The pores help to keep the skin moist. They connect with the *nephridia* which excrete liquid wastes collected in the

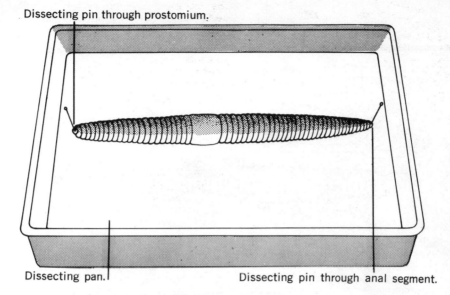

Dissecting pin through prostomium.

Dissecting pan.

Dissecting pin through anal segment.

Fig. 4. Arranging Specimen for Dissection.

coelomic cavity. (See Fig. 13.) The pores can be seen with the aid of a hand lens or with a dissecting microscope. Nearer to the anterior (front) end than to the posterior (back) end of the worm is a thick cylindrical collar (*clitellum*) which is used in reproduction. The worm's protective coating (*cuticle*) which is a secretion of the skin, is kept moist by special mucus glands. Each segment (*somite*) is partially separated from its neighbor by a thin wall called the *septum*. The fleshy lobe (*prostomium*) over the mouth is not considered a segment of the earthworm. It serves to give a cushioning effect to the sensory endings of the earthworm.

Arranging Specimen for Dissection

Now we are ready to dissect and study the internal anatomy of the earthworm. Place the specimen on the dissecting pan with its ventral side down. Extend the specimen to form a straight line. Put a dissecting pin through the prostomium and another through the *anal segment* (see Fig. 4). To dissect the worm follow directions in Figs. 5, 6, 7, 8 and 9.

17

Step 1. With forceps gently lift skin at about 2″ from clitellum.

Step. 2. With razor blade make slight cut at point A.

Step. 3. Insert sharp end of scissors. Cut through skin toward anus, slightly to one side of dorsal midline, to point B. Be careful to cut through skin only, no deeper.

Step 4. Make similar cut in opposite direction until you get to about 1″ from clitellum.

Fig. 5. Exposing Internal Structures of Earthworm.

Step 5. Use forceps to hold body wall as shown.

Step 6. Beginning at anus, cut through septa on each side of intestine with sharp tipped scalpel or razor blade. Continue detaching intestine to within one inch of clitellum.

Fig. 6. Cutting Septa On Each Side of Intestine.

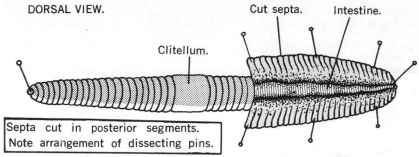

DORSAL VIEW.

Clitellum.

Cut septa.   Intestine.

Septa cut in posterior segments.
Note arrangement of dissecting pins.

Fig. 7. Intestinal Region of Earthworm.

Step 1. Cut through clitellum and up to prostomium as shown by dotted line. Do not cut deeper than through body wall.

Step 2. Sever the septa as in Fig. 6.

Step 3. Roll back body wall; pin each side to dissecting pan to expose all organs as in Fig. 9.

Fig. 8. Exposing Internal Organs from Clitellum to Mouth.

The Digestive System

Fig. 9 shows only the digestive system of the earthworm, with all other internal organs omitted. This diagram will help you to identify the parts of the digestive system in the specimen.

Typhlosole and Intestine

The upper part of the intestine contains a tube called the *typhlosole* (see Fig. 10) that increases the surface area of the intestine so that it can absorb and digest more food. The typhlosole is like a tube within a tube.

19

Mouth — located under prostomium.

Muscular pharynx — for drawing in food and swallowing.

Esophagus — narrow passage between pharynx and crop.

Large thin-walled crop — for temporary food storage.

Muscular gizzard — to grind food with aid of earth grains.

Anus — wastes are expelled here.

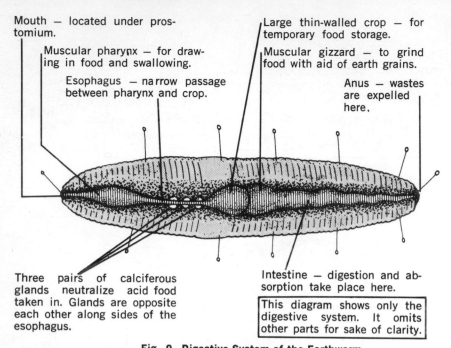

Three pairs of calciferous glands neutralize acid food taken in. Glands are opposite each other along sides of the esophagus.

Intestine — digestion and absorption take place here.

This diagram shows only the digestive system. It omits other parts for sake of clarity.

Fig. 9. Digestive System of the Earthworm.

Fig. 10. Arrangement of Typhlosole Within Intestine — Schematic Diagram.

Typhlosole.

Intestine.

Coelom.

Segments cut away to show extension of typhlosole and intestine.

Body wall.

Segments.

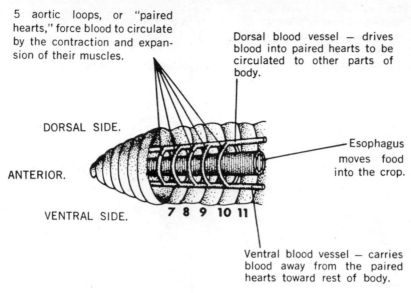

5 aortic loops, or "paired hearts," force blood to circulate by the contraction and expansion of their muscles.

Dorsal blood vessel — drives blood into paired hearts to be circulated to other parts of body.

DORSAL SIDE.

ANTERIOR.

VENTRAL SIDE.

7 8 9 10 11

Esophagus moves food into the crop.

Ventral blood vessel — carries blood away from the paired hearts toward rest of body.

Fig. 11. The Paired Hearts of the Earthworm.

The Circulatory System

The circulatory system of the earthworm is complicated. The earthworm has "five pairs of hearts" located in segments 7 through 11 (see Fig. 11). They pump the blood by muscular contractions. The hearts may be seen pulsing in a living earthworm if the worm is held up to the light and gently squeezed. The animal has several large blood vessels and many smaller blood vessels. It also contains numerous microscopic blood vessels called *capillaries.*

Study the diagram in Fig. 11 (Paired Hearts of the Earthworm) and in Fig. 12 (Major Blood Vessels of the Earthworm) to locate the hearts and blood vessels in the dissected specimen. The larger blood vessels are readily identifiable; other smaller vessels such as the *integumental vessels* which supply the circulatory needs of the skin are hard to find. Every part of the earthworm is richly supplied with blood vessels. The blood vessels are paired, one for the parts of the body on the left side of the worm and the other for corresponding parts on the right side. Each blood vessel carries blood to or from particular structures or organs.

21

Typical segment in intestinal region showing location and function of main blood vessels.

Dorsal vessel.   Intestine.

Intestinal vein carries blood away from intestines.

Parietal vein returns blood from the body wall.

Intestinal artery supplies blood to intestine.

Parietal artery supplies blood to cells in body wall.

Lateral neural vessel supplies segmental nerves.

Nerve trunk transmits nerve impulses to and from the brain and helps coordinate segmental responses.

Sub neural vessel supplies the nerve cord.

Nerve trunk.   Ventral vessel.

Fig. 12. Major Blood Vessels of Earthworm—Schematic Diagram.

The Excretory System—The Sanitation Department

The earthworm, like all other animals including humans, has to dispose of three types of wastes—solid matter, liquid wastes and gaseous wastes. The solid wastes or feces are expelled through the anus. The liquid wastes and part of the gaseous wastes are removed from the coelomic cavity with the aid of special coiled pipes called nephridia (see Fig. 13). One coiled pipe is a *nephridium.*

Nephridia in the earthworm are found in all but the first three segments and in the last one. Each segment contains a pair of nephridia. You may easily identify them in your specimen by examining the rear, or posterior segments, where there are few structures to confuse the dissector.

Examine the diagram of the nephridia in Fig. 13 and trace a nephridium in the specimen from its opening in one segment to its connection with a pore in the skin of the next

Nephridium — removes liquid waste from body cavity or coelom.

DORSAL SIDE.

Dorsal vessel.

Typhlosole.

Intestine.

Body wall.

Coelom.

Pore — Enables liquid wastes to leave body

Ventral vessel.

Lateral neural vessel.

Nerve trunk.

Subneural vessel.

Liquid in coelom or body cavity.

Ciliated funnel of nephridium. Movement of cilia creates current driving coelomic fluid into the nephridium.

VENTRAL SIDE.

Arrows show direction coelomic liquid flows, from ciliated funnel through and out of a pore in the skin. It carries with it liquid wastes of the body.

Fig. 13. Cross Section of an Earthworm Through Intestinal Region Emphasizing the Nephridia.

segment. Use your magnifying lens to explore the nephridial or excretory system. Note that the nephridium has one opening at the ciliated funnel which collects liquid wastes from the coelom and another opening at the pore through which liquid wastes leave the body.

The Reproductive System—Starting the Next Generation

The earthworm, like most animals, has sex organs. The main function of these organs is to produce sex cells—sperm cells by the male organs and egg cells by the female organs. The union of a sperm cell with an egg cell starts a number of cell divisions and chemical changes that finally result in the formation of new animals—the next generation.

MALE ORGANS:

Sperm sac.

Testis sac. Testes within sac produce sperm cells.

Sperm receptacle temporarily stores sperm cells from testis, then discharges them through sperm duct.

Testis sac.

Sperm duct.

Sperm cells move from testes along sperm duct, through opening in cuticle, along mucus secretion to clitellum.

Opening through cuticle. Sperm cells discharged here during mating to unite with egg cells and fertilize them.

9

10

11

12

13

14

15

FEMALE ORGANS:

Ovary containing eggs.

Funnel for receiving eggs.

Egg sac.

Oviduct.

Opening through cuticle. Egg cells discharged here during mating.

Dorsal view of segments 9-15 showing only reproductive structures most readily seen during dissection.

Fig. 14. Reproductive System of Earthworm.

Unlike many animals, each earthworm contains both male and female sex organs. There are no earthworms that are solely female or male, yet each earthworm needs to mate with another earthworm. There is no contact between the egg cells and sperm cells within a single earthworm. The sperm cells are not discharged unless mating between two earthworms takes place.

The sex organs of the earthworm are described in Fig. 14. It takes an experienced and skillful dissector to expose and identify all the parts of the reproductive system because some

24

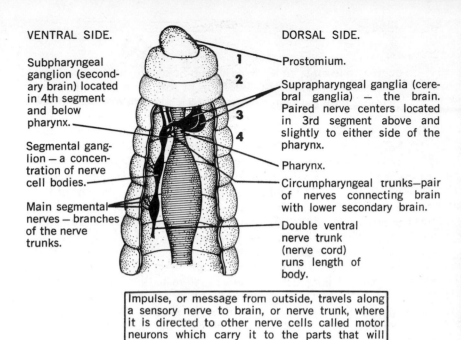

VENTRAL SIDE.

Subpharyngeal ganglion (secondary brain) located in 4th segment and below pharynx.

Segmental ganglion — a concentration of nerve cell bodies.

Main segmental nerves — branches of the nerve trunks.

DORSAL SIDE.

1 — Prostomium.

2 — Suprapharyngeal ganglia (cerebral ganglia) — the brain. Paired nerve centers located in 3rd segment above and slightly to either side of the pharynx.

3

4 — Pharynx.

Circumpharyngeal trunks—pair of nerves connecting brain with lower secondary brain.

Double ventral nerve trunk (nerve cord) runs length of body.

Impulse, or message from outside, travels along a sensory nerve to brain, or nerve trunk, where it is directed to other nerve cells called motor neurons which carry it to the parts that will react, i.e., muscles or glands.

Fig. 15. Nervous System of Earthworm—Simplified Pattern.

of the parts are inside other parts. However, by studying Fig. 14, which shows only the main parts, you will be able to get a good idea of the structure of the reproductive system.

The Clitellum as a Nest

The clitellum, which is formed around several segments in preparation for the process of reproduction, forms a cocoon that encases the developing worms. Later in the reproductive process the clitellum is slipped off the body of the worm much as a ring is slipped off a finger. After it has slipped over the anterior end of the worm, a mucus secretion from the skin cells seals each end of the clitellum, forming a protective nest for the developing worms until they are ready to leave their temporary home.

The Nervous System of the Earthworm—Keeping in Touch

It may be surprising to learn that the lowly worm has a brain. Of course it is not as magnificent nor as complex as man's brain but it does enable the earthworm, to a limited

25

degree, to learn from its experiences. Scientific researchers have proved this by testing the behavior of earthworms in a maze, a chamber with pathways designed to lead to an exit (escape or reward chamber) or to one or more dead ends. (See Fig. 17.)

Just what is a brain? It is a center of nerve cells that helps to coordinate the activities of an animal. In the earthworm the brain is connected with the *double ventral nerve cord.* (See Fig. 15.) The brain and trunk lines have nerves which branch off to all parts of the body. Thus any part of the worm affected by something outside itself may send a message to other parts of the body, such as the segmental muscles and the setae. The worm can then retreat to the safety of its burrow. This communication system helps the worm to survive, that is, to get food and to escape its enemies.

In any animal the nervous system is the most difficult to dissect. This is equally true for the earthworm. Fig. 15 is a simplified diagram of the worm's nervous system. Study this diagram. Then, with the aid of your magnifying lens or dissecting microscope, locate the labeled parts in your specimen.

At the beginning of the dissection (Fig. 5) you were cautioned not to cut too deeply into the specimen, especially in the anterior region. Now you can see why this is so important. It is very easy to destroy the brain or the nerve centers by careless dissection.

The organ systems in the earthworm are much simpler than those of animals more commonly used in projects and experiments, such as frogs, mice or guinea pigs. Therefore the results obtained in experiments with earthworms are often more easily understood than are results from experiments with higher animals.

Earthworms are excellent for many kinds of projects and experiments. They are relatively easy to keep alive in the home or in the laboratory. They take up little space and do not create a mess that requires frequent cleaning. As long as they are kept moist there is little danger of injuring the worms by handling. Here are some interesting experiments and projects to try with earthworms.

Project 1: Demonstrating the Beating Hearts of the Earthworm

Obtain two six-inch squares of ordinary window pane glass. Place a quarter-inch layer of vaseline along all four

Step 1. Prepare glass square with vaseline along edges as shown.

Step 2. Place live earthworm within vaseline edges of square. Vaseline forms a seal between 2 glass squares (see Step 3) and prevents worm from escaping.

Step 3. Quickly cover earthworm with second glass square to hold worm between the 2 squares.

Step 4. Gently press glass squares together to squeeze worm's body into an almost oval shape.

Step 5. Hold squares in front of strong light to see beating hearts of the worm.

Fig. 16. Method of Studying Beating Hearts of Earthworm.

edges of one glass square. Place a live earthworm within the vaseline-edged square as shown in Fig. 16, and follow the instructions in Fig. 16. When you have completed this experiment, examine the specimen between the glass squares with your hand lens or dissecting microscope to get an enlarged view of the beating hearts.

Many different and exciting experiments may be developed using the same technique as that used to demonstrate the beating hearts. For example, you can study the effects of hormones such as adrenin (adrenalin) and insulin on the heartbeat of the worm. Keep the worm for a short time on a moist surface, such as a blotter, saturated with a solution of the substance whose effects are being studied. Then transfer the worm to the glass squares and observe the effects of the chemical on the worm. In this way you can study the possible effects of such chemical substances as aspirin, alcohol, ascorbic acid, glutathione, thyroid extract, auxin, gibberellic acid, etc. on the circulatory system of the earthworm.

Project 2: Investigating Sex Cells of an Earthworm

The sperm cells of the earthworm can be studied under a microscope having at least 400x magnification. This project requires slides, cover slips, a *Syracuse dish* or *Petri dish* and a medicine dropper, as well as dissecting instruments.

Obtain live earthworms from a biological supply house or collect them yourself. Live worms are most easily collected after a heavy rain when they come out of their burrows. The worms can be put under anaesthesia by immersing them in a 5% urethane-water solution for five minutes. Dissect out the sperm sacs and testes by following the procedure described in Figs. 5, 6, 7 and 8. (Consult Fig. 14 to help locate the sperm sacs and testes.) Place them in the Syracuse dish or Petri dish. Add a few drops of water to the dish. Break up the structure of the sperm sacs and testes with a pair of dissecting needles. Now draw up several drops of the mixture with a medicine dropper and transfer one drop to a microscope slide. Examine the drop with the microscope to find the living sperm cells. This whole process should be accomplished quickly because the cells do not remain alive for long.

You can also examine the egg cells of the earthworm under a microscope. Follow the same procedure as described for obtaining sperm cells but dissect out the ovaries instead. Consult the diagram of the reproductive system (Fig. 14) to help you locate the ovaries.

It would be most interesting to try to fertilize the egg cells of one earthworm with the sperm cells of another by removing them from earthworms as described above and placing the egg and sperm cells in a dish containing Ringer's solution for cold-blooded animals. Consult your science teacher or any text on physiology, to get information on the preparation of Ringer's solution.

Studies of the reproduction and development of worms may be done by dissecting the clitellums of worms of different lengths. Small worms are generally not as likely to have fertilizations as are the mature worms. A study of the cocoons of worms may be made, to observe different stages in the de-

28

Exposed wires. When worm crawls across wires, current passes through it and shocks worm, in addition to irritation felt when moving over the coarse sandpaper.

Sandpaper.

Possible routes.

Out.

Out.

Walls of maze made of plywood or masonite.

Earthworm has a choice of going to left or right. After many trials and many shocks it learns to go only to the right.

1.5 volt dry cell battery.

In.

Fig. 17. The Yerkes Maze—To Study Behavior of Earthworm.

velopment of young worms. It is also possible to do experiments on *parthenogenesis*, that is, fertilizing an egg cell *without* a sperm cell. One method that has been used in parthenogenesis experiments is to pierce the egg's membrane gently with a fine glass needle or a metal needle.

Project 3: A Study of Behavior—The Worm Turns

You can study the learning ability of the earthworm by repeating or modifying the maze experiments performed by Yerkes and Heck (see Fig. 17). They discovered some interesting things about the earthworm's ability to profit from experience. In a series of experiments they removed the "brain" or cerebral ganglia of earthworms. When they tested these worms in the maze the results were surprising!

An interesting variation of the maze experiment would be a study of the reactions of the earthworm in a similar maze, using a blotter saturated with a harmless acid like acetic acid or vinegar instead of the electric shock method. No doubt you will think of many other interesting behavior experiments with earthworms.

Project 4: We Can Cultivate Earthworms

It is quite easy to maintain earthworms in a special bedding material called "Buss" bedder—a commercial product. Once you have succeeded in raising some worms, it is possible to introduce various chemicals into the bedding compound to test the effects of these chemicals on the growth, reproduction and behavior of the earthworm. Test the effects of such chemicals as tryptophan, nucleic acid, thyroxin, cytosine, riboflavin, alpha tocopherol (Vitamin E), ascorbic acid and many others.

The earthworm is made up of many similar segments with little specialization to differentiate one segment from another. It does not even have a distinct head. In higher animals you will see the segments become specialized, with well-developed appendages and definite body divisions, including a head equipped with a complicated brain and sense organs. Thus the earthworm presents the simplified evolutionary pattern of the structure of higher invertebrate animals. We can think of the earthworm's pattern of structure as Nature's living clay from which was molded more advanced forms of invertebrate life.

Project 5: The Effects of Pesticides on Earthworm Ecology

Is the beneficial value of earthworms lost or diminished when man uses insecticides or fungicides to control plant pests? Let's find out. Procedure: (see Project 4). Add "Buss" bedder to 6 plastic (not metal) seedling trays with drainage holes. Place 3 earthworms in each tray. Wrap plastic screening around each tray to prevent their escaping. Maintain earthworms for a week to establish a normal pattern of life.

Obtain commonly used pesticides, such as malathion, sevin, nicotine sulfate, etc. from a hardware store or plant nursery. Use spray cans or mix small amounts, following the directions on the cans, and put in a hand spray gun. Allow 2 trays to act as controls, i.e. add no chemicals to them. Spray each of the other four trays with a different pesticide, as though they were plants. Handling the worms with rubber gloves, examine them daily with a stereomicroscope (10x to 100x) or hand lens for possible changes in heartbeat, skin color, and behavior.

Select one worm from each tray every third day, immerse in alcohol, and perform an autopsy. Look for comparative size of organs, such as gonads, intestine, etc. Evaluate results.

Animals with Armor — 3
The Crayfish

IN CHAPTER 2 we dissected a simple, segmented animal, the earthworm, a creature without any protective armor. Now we shall work with a crayfish, an animal that is related to the simple earthworm. The crayfish, however, has specialized segments with a tough suit of armor and external appendages, or limbs. It uses its limbs for fighting, for food getting, for locomotion and so on.

If a crayfish were enlarged to the size of a dinosaur like the *Tyrannosaurus* it would appear far more terrifying than the dinosaur. Imagine a creature with gigantic crushing pincers, with long waving antennae searching for victims, with powerful crushing jaws—a monster equipped with a thick wall of heavy armor in the form of an outer skeleton. Fortunately the crayfish grows to only about 5 inches in length. Its relative, the lobster, can grow about 2 feet long and be quite formidable.

The crayfish is a scavenger. It lives on the muddy bottoms of streams and ponds, emerging at night to feed on dead matter, live insect larvae and worms. It is often cannibalistic. Racoons, fresh water bass, muskrats, crows and man are among its mortal enemies. To escape its foes it flexes its tail, the *uropod*, spreads it like a fan and draws it forward underneath its body w.... a strong motion. This causes the crayfish to dart backwards into the muddy bottom which is further stirred by its rapid motion. His enemies generally lose him in the muddied water.

The tiny crayfish can cause enormous damage. It burrows several feet deep into the bottoms of streams, especially near overhanging banks. These innumerable burrows, frequently

Fig. 18. Large Crayfish (Cambarus).
Courtesy Carolina Biological Supply Company.

enlarged by muskrats, weaken dikes or levees, and serious floods may develop.

Some gill breathing cousins of the crayfish are lobsters, crabs, shrimps, prawns, barnacles and krill. The *Crustacea,* the group to which all of these belong, are an important food source for man. Lobsters, crabs, shrimps, prawns and crayfish are eaten by man. Prawns resemble shrimps except for a little hump on their *cephalothorax* or back. In fact the "shrimp" that you eat in a shrimp salad may have been sold to your local fish market by a "prawn broker." You would not know the difference.

Barnacles, a variety of crustacea, do great damage to our ships and wharves. A shrimp-like crustacean commonly called krill or whale food is estimated to produce over a billion tons of food for whales each year. Scientists have been thinking of using krill to supplement the food resources of man.

The outer skeleton or *exoskeleton* of the crayfish and of other invertebrates consists mainly of a tough substance called *chitin.* (See Project 1 in this chapter.) It is a very effective protection but it also imprisons the growing crayfish. In order to grow, the crayfish must escape from its exoskeletal prison. This it does by molting, or shedding, its outer skeleton. The exoskeleton splits at a crease in the cephalothorax (see Fig. 19) and the crayfish squeezes out of the exoskeleton, sometimes leaving behind a leg as well as the shell. Thus defenceless, it hides until it grows a larger exoskeleton. Often, to escape an enemy, the crayfish will snap off its own leg if the enemy

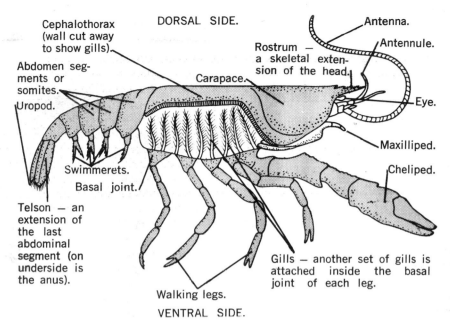

Fig. 19. External Anatomy of Crayfish.

is holding it. The crayfish has the power to regenerate, or grow back another leg if it has lost one.

The crayfish can walk backward, forward and even sideways because it has 7 joints in each walking leg, each joint arranged in a different position. Abdominal appendages called *swimmerets* help to keep the animal clean. The first two swimmerets in the male are modified to form channels for transporting sperm cells to the female. In the female the eggs, which look like clusters of grapes, are attached to the swimmerets at egg-laying time. They remain attached to the outside of the swimmerets until the developing crayfish have grown large enough to achieve independence from the mother crayfish.

Like the earthworm, the crayfish is built on the segment plan. However, the crayfish is a more advanced animal than the earthworm. Therefore, its segments are not all alike. While the earthworm has primitive structures called setae, the crayfish has specialized appendages such as swimmerets, walking legs, antennae, etc. (See Fig. 19.) Instead of a pair of nephridia in each segment, as in the earthworm, we find in the crayfish a single excretory organ. The nervous system and the digestive system in the crayfish resemble those of the earthworm. But unlike those of the earthworm, the sense organs of the crayfish, such as eyes and antennae, are well developed. The earthworm has only light-sensitive spots in its head and no antennae, while the crayfish has large compound eyes, each eye made up of about 2500 sections, and large antennae resembling those of the grasshopper.

Preparing for the Dissection

The crayfish dissection will show how the structure of a more complicated invertebrate, like the crayfish, is built on the simple foundation of the earthworm's plan of structure. It will also show dramatically how the higher forms have added to and altered the simple segment plan of the earthworm.

Let's see what we are going to need for this dissection. First, order two injected crayfish, type *Astacus fluviatilis*, at least 3 inches long. Then obtain a pair of sharp, curved scissors about 4 inches long, and the same equipment as listed for the earthworm dissection.

External Features of the Crayfish

Place the specimen on its side in the dissecting pan, as shown in Fig. 19. Do not use any dissecting pins at this time. We will study first the external features of the crayfish. Examine the dorsal surface and locate the two main body divisions, the *cephalothorax* (fused segments of the head and thorax) and the *abdomen*. Note segments in abdomen. Now examine one side and the ventral surface of the specimen. Identify structures labeled in Fig. 19. Note the different types of appendages—antennae, antennules, mouth parts, legs and swimmerets.

Directions for Exposing Gills of Crayfish

Before exposing the crayfish's gills, remove the legs and swimmerets from abdomen and thorax region by cutting through the first or basal joint near body. Follow directions in Fig. 20 and cut away a section of the *carapace* (exoskeleton covering the head-thorax region).

How does the attachment of the gills to the legs help the crayfish in breathing? (See Fig. 21.) When the legs move, the gills attached to the legs move in a waving motion like a flag on a flagpole. This waving motion stirs the water which enters under the carapace. Since water contains dissolved oxygen (O_2)

34

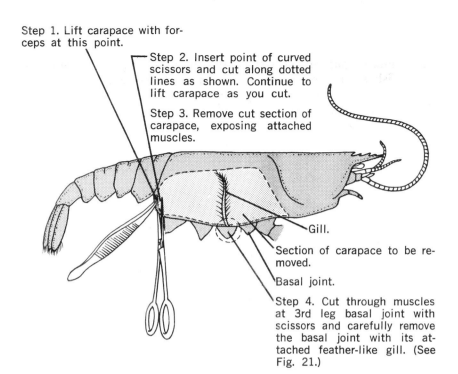

Step 1. Lift carapace with forceps at this point.

Step 2. Insert point of curved scissors and cut along dotted lines as shown. Continue to lift carapace as you cut.

Step 3. Remove cut section of carapace, exposing attached muscles.

Gill.

Section of carapace to be removed.

Basal joint.

Step 4. Cut through muscles at 3rd leg basal joint with scissors and carefully remove the basal joint with its attached feather-like gill. (See Fig. 21.)

Fig. 20. Exposing Gills of Crayfish.

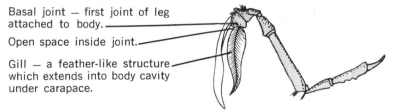

Basal joint — first joint of leg attached to body.

Open space inside joint.

Gill — a feather-like structure which extends into body cavity under carapace.

Fig. 21. Walking Leg of Crayfish Showing Gill Attachment.

the stirring of the water brings the O_2 to the blood canals in the gills where absorption of O_2 into the bloodstream takes place.

Dorsal View of Crayfish

You have just examined the crayfish from a side view. Now let us study its dorsal side. We can expose several important organs and blood vessels by cutting a long, narrow section of the exoskeleton from the dorsal side of the crayfish. Place the crayfish in the dissecting pan, dorsal side up. Now study Fig. 22 and follow directions for the dissection.

35

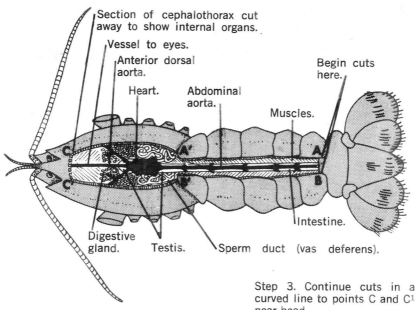

Section of cephalothorax cut away to show internal organs.

Vessel to eyes.

Anterior dorsal aorta.

Heart.

Abdominal aorta.

Muscles.

Begin cuts here.

Intestine.

Digestive gland.

Testis.

Sperm duct (vas deferens).

Step 1. Using forceps, gently lift hard outer layer at points A and B in front of tail.

Step 2. Cut across from A to B and from points A and B cut forward to points A^1 and B^1.

Step 3. Continue cuts in a curved line to points C and C^1 near head.

Step 4. Cut from point C to C^1. Then lift and remove the cut section of the exoskeleton.

Step 5. Locate and identify all parts labeled here.

Fig. 22. Dorsal View of Internal Organs of Crayfish.

Do not remove the mouth parts until you have studied the organ systems. (See Figs. 22, 23 and 24 for locating these systems—the nervous, excretory and circulatory systems.) You may damage the organ systems unless you acquaint yourself with their relation to the mouth parts.

Internal Organs of Crayfish

We are now ready to explore the internal anatomy of the crayfish. The most complicated system in the crayfish is its circulatory system. This is illustrated in Fig. 24 and will be described in detail later. The other systems of the crayfish are fairly simple and are very much like the systems in the earthworm, except for the excretory system. All the main systems, except the circulatory system, are shown in Fig. 23.

Exposing Main Organ Systems of the Crayfish

Using small curved scissors, cut away the basal joints to which the legs were attached. (See Fig 20.) Now remove

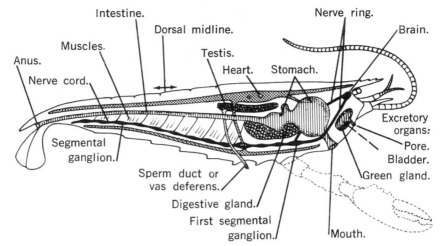

Fig. 23. Side View of Internal Organs of Crayfish.

with scissors all gills in the section of the cephalothorax which was previously opened. Examine the gills with a hand lens to observe how they are adapted for getting oxygen into the blood. They are very thin and feathery, offering a great deal of surface for taking in oxygen from the water.

Carefully lift and cut away hard outer protective plates from dorsal midline to base of each leg. Use forceps to lift and hold the plates from the dorsal midline as you cut to the base of each leg. Use forceps and probe to remove masses of muscle from the region of the eyes down to the last walking leg on the side being dissected. Then cut away the skeletal plates down to the tail to expose the abdomen. As you lift and cut muscles, watch to see whether you are cutting into any other organs. Avoid damaging any parts of the systems shown in Fig. 23.

With a fine probe, trace the body systems in the following order: *a.* the excretory system (near the mouth), *b.* the digestive system, *c.* the reproductive system and *d.* the nervous system.

How does the nervous system of the crayfish compare with the nervous system of the earthworm?

Circulatory System of Crayfish

Now that the crayfish has been opened we can study the circulatory system and locate the heart and the main blood vessels. Arrows in Fig. 24 show direction of blood flow to and

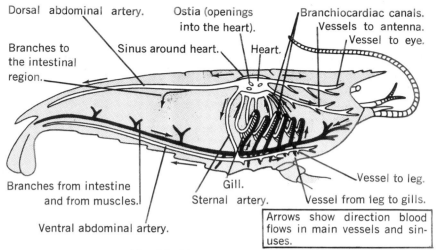

Dorsal abdominal artery.

Ostia (openings into the heart).

Branchiocardiac canals.

Vessels to antenna.

Vessel to eye.

Branches to the intestinal region.

Sinus around heart.

Heart.

Branches from intestine and from muscles.

Gill.

Sternal artery.

Ventral abdominal artery.

Vessel to leg.

Vessel from leg to gills.

Arrows show direction blood flows in main vessels and sinuses.

Fig. 24. Circulatory System of Crayfish.

from the heart. Locate in the specimen the main vessels labeled in Fig. 24. There are no veins in the crayfish. Blood flows from heart to arteries to capillaries and then into tissue spaces called *sinuses* which serve in place of veins. The sinuses around the gills are called canals. Blood sinuses are also found in insects. Man has blood sinuses in the liver. He has hollows in the facial bones which are also called sinuses. If these become infected, we suffer from what is popularly known as a "sinus attack."

Appendages of the Crayfish

The word "appendages" generally means limbs, such as arms, wings, legs or fins. Scientifically, appendages are all movable structures that extend outward from the body of an animal regardless of the part of the animal to which the extension is attached. In the crayfish the antennae, antennules and other parts attached to the head and abdomen are appendages. Each has an important function and all appendages are controlled by the nervous system. They govern the senses of touch and taste and they help the crayfish to breathe and to chew its food.

We shall now dissect and examine the appendages of the head. (See Fig. 25.) First free the mouth parts from the head with sharp-tipped scalpel, scissors and forceps. Then dissect out the antennae by holding them with forceps and cutting a shallow groove into the head where the antennae are attached.

This will free the antennae. Find the nerve and blood vessel attachments to these parts. The nerves look like thin white cords. Study the mouth parts with a hand lens or dissecting microscope, and with a probe find out how they are arranged to carry out their functions.

Use a hand lens or dissecting microscope to study appendages. Study the table in Fig. 25 to understand how the design of each structure helps it to do its job effectively.

With a hand lens find the blood vessels in a detached walking leg. Note how the gill is attached to the leg (see Fig. 21). The open space in the leg is part of a blood sinus.

Now that you've come this far, try your hand at the following projects. The purpose of these projects is to provide interpretive experiences for the reader, experiences that can only be really fulfilled by actual comparative dissections and by the analysis of comparable parts.

Project 1: Behind the Chitin Curtain

Chitin is the horny substance that forms the hard outer shell of the crayfish and of other crustaceans and insects. Let's find out what's behind it. We can begin to understand the evolutionary changes in the structure of crustaceans by making a comparative study of the lobster, shrimp and barnacle.

Obtain injected specimens of these animals. Compare their external organization with that of the crayfish. Do the same with the internal organization, after the specimens have been dissected. If you run into difficulty, you might consult your biology teacher or refer to a book on invertebrate zoology.

Assemble the mouth parts of each specimen and show how they compare in structure and function with the mouth parts of the crayfish. Observe how the crustacean pattern of structure has been modified in the barnacle. How have these changes helped the barnacle to survive?

Project 2: Making a Photographic Study of Appendages

Many science magazines are anxious to get unusual nature pictures for their natural history features. They pay well. Perhaps you can do some profitable free-lance nature photography.

Dissect out and photograph the appendages of crustaceans (limbs, mouth parts, etc.). Arrange these photographs in order so that similar structures in the different animals such

FIG. 25. APPENDAGES OF THE CRAYFISH AND THEIR FUNCTIONS.

APPENDAGES OF CEPHALOTHORAX
(HEAD AND THORAX)

APPENDAGE:		FUNCTION:	LOCATION:
Antennules.		Detects touch and taste. Helps to balance crayfish.	Front of mouth.
Antenna.		Detects touch and taste.	Front of mouth.
Mandbile or jaw.		Crushes food.	Mouth.
First maxilla.		Moves food to mouth.	Behind mandibles.
Second maxilla.		Bails water in gill chamber.	Behind mandibles.
First maxilliped.		Holds food. Touch. Taste.	At forward and ventral part of thorax region.

	Second maxilliped.	Holds food. Touch. Taste.	At forward and ventral part of thorax region.
	Third maxilliped.	Holds food. Touch. Taste.	At forward and ventral part of thorax region.
	Walking leg, four on each side.	For locomotion.	Posterior to maxillipeds at ventral part of thorax.
	Cheliped, the first leg.	To grasp food.	Posterior to maxillipeds at ventral part of thorax.

APPENDAGES OF THE ABDOMEN

	Swimmeret.	First swimmeret in male transfers sperm to female who uses 2nd, 3rd, 4th and 5th swimmerets to hold eggs and young.	Abdominal region on ventral side.
	Uropod.	For swimming.	Tail end.

as mandibles, appendages and so on, may be compared. For instance, the photographs of the mandibles of these organisms should be set side by side.

Project 3:   New Parts for Old

Do you want to create new animals from old parts? Try your hand at experiments on regeneration. Regeneration is the ability of some animals to grow back a lost part of the body. Animals which have been used successfully in experiments on regeneration are tadpoles, salamanders, earthworms, planaria, crayfish and hydra.

Try testing the effects of such chemicals as glutamic acid and acetylcholine on regeneration by adding these chemicals to the water in which the animals are kept. Several biological supply houses have printed material available on the subject of regeneration.

Project 4:   Home Life of the Crayfish

Study the crayfish in its natural surroundings or habitat. Record your observations of its movements, the food it eats and how it reproduces itself. City folks rarely get to see crayfish in their natural surroundings. However, even city folk can study the life of a crayfish in an aquarium.

It is possible to set up an aquarium at home or school and observe the development of young crayfish in it. For your aquarium use pond water, water plants and a bottom consisting of gravel, earth and small stones. Arrange the bottom so that there are miniature steep banks. Add maggots and other food to the water. Stock the tank with snails, small fresh water clams and small fish.

Before we move on to the next dissection, let us stop to consider what we have accomplished. We have learned how to dissect, what instruments to use and how to use them. We have dissected a simple, spineless animal, the earthworm. This gives us some idea of what a primitive animal is like. We moved onward to dissect the crayfish, an animal linked by distant kinship to the earthworm and by closer kinship to the most advanced forms of invertebrates, the insects. Let's now go on to examine the grasshopper, one example of an advanced form of invertebrate.

Danger — Grasshopper 4

GRASSHOPPERS are found almost everywhere. They will eat practically any wild or cultivated plant. In some areas of the United States special contraptions called hopperdozers have been used to catch grasshoppers in cultivated fields. Hopperdozers have caught as many as a million and a half grasshoppers per acre. Just imagine how many grasshoppers there must be in the whole United States!

A grasshopper cannot eat much by itself. But it has been estimated that 17 grasshoppers per square yard, on a forty acre field, can eat one ton of alfalfa hay in one day! Multiply that figure by the millions of acres of farm land, and the possible destruction of crops becomes alarming. That is why we started by saying "Danger—Grasshopper."

The Top of the Invertebrate Ladder—the Insects

The grasshopper belongs to the highest and most complicated group of invertebrate animals, the insects. If we compare our old friend, the earthworm with the grasshopper, we can quickly see how much they resemble each other. For example, the grasshopper's body, like the body of the earthworm, is arranged in segments. The earthworm has paired appendages (the setae) attached to its segments. The grasshopper also has paired appendages attached to its segments. However, the grasshopper's appendages are naturally more complicated and more specialized.

The earthworm appeared on earth much earlier than the grasshopper. In fact, the earthworm and its kin were at one time the highest form of animal life on earth. In the previous chapter we examined and dissected a crayfish. We could see how the crayfish is descended from the earthworm. Actually,

Fig. 26. Wingless Grasshopper (Romalea microptera).
Courtesy American Museum of Natural History.

in evolutionary development, the crayfish and its cousins are sandwiched between the primitive earthworm and the advanced insects. The anatomy of the grasshopper shows this evolutionary development more clearly than do many other animals.

Thus far, we have mentioned only the external features that relate the earthworm to the crayfish and the grasshopper. To better understand the close ties among these animals we must penetrate their chitin overcoats (exoskeletons) by dissecting them. We can then see how the different systems, such as the digestive, circulatory, nervous and other systems of these groups compare with each other.

Count Down for Dissection

This dissection requires several injected specimens of the Carolina grasshopper, *Dissosteira carolina,* or *Romalea microptera,* which is a larger type. Get at least two males and two females because this is a difficult dissection. In addition to the equipment used for dissecting the earthworm, we will need a pair of small scissors with fine, straight blades about 2½ inches long, and a narrow tipped medicine dropper about 3 inches long.

External Anatomy of the Grasshopper

Before we dissect the grasshopper, let's study Fig. 27 and acquaint ourselves with the external characteristics. Locate the three main body divisions on your specimen—abdomen, thorax, head. Notice the segmented character of the body.

44

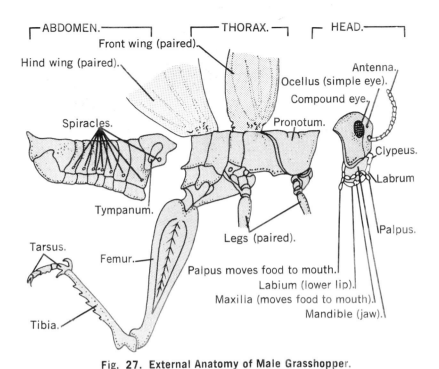

Fig. 27. External Anatomy of Male Grasshopper.

Fig. 28. Face View of Male Grasshopper's Head.

PART:	FUNCTION:
Labial palpi	Sense of smell and touch.
Labium	Helps hold food to be chewed.
Maxillary palpi	Sense of smell and touch.
Maxillae	Helps grind food.
Labrum (upper lip)	Helps hold food to be chewed.
Mandibles (jaws)	Crush food.
Tongue (hypopharynx)	Probably provides taste sensation.

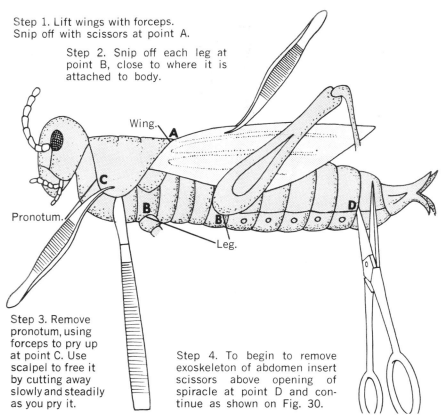

Step 1. Lift wings with forceps. Snip off with scissors at point A.

Step 2. Snip off each leg at point B, close to where it is attached to body.

Wing.

Pronotum.

Leg.

Step 3. Remove pronotum, using forceps to pry up at point C. Use scalpel to free it by cutting away slowly and steadily as you pry it.

Step 4. To begin to remove exoskeleton of abdomen insert scissors above opening of spiracle at point D and continue as shown on Fig. 30.

Fig. 29. Beginning Dissection of Female Grasshopper.

Identify all parts of abdomen and thorax shown in Fig. 27. Use hand lens to see the spiracles in the abdomen.

How many pairs of legs does the grasshopper have? How many did the crayfish have? A good principle to remember is that the more advanced an animal is, the fewer appendages it has, either in its adult or its embryonic stage.

Examine the wings with a hand lens. As in most insects there are two pairs of wings. The arrangement of the veins in the wings is *inherited* and is different in each insect. Examine the head with a hand lens. The head is really a fusion of the first six segments. Identify each part of the head as labeled in Fig. 28.

Dissecting the Grasshopper

Figs. 29 and 30 give directions for all the steps in dissecting the exoskeleton. The first steps in this dissection are

46

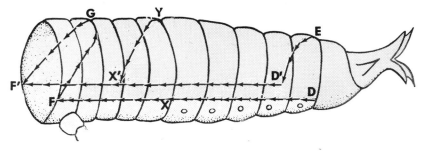

Step 5. Cut from point D to E and continue down on other side to D¹. Make all incisions shallow.

Step 6. Then cut from point D to F and from F to G, and continue down on other side to F¹.

Step 7. Cut from point D¹ to F¹ on the other side of body.

Step 8. Now cut from X to Y and continue down on other side to X¹. The exoskeleton is now divided into 2 cut sections, F to X, and X to D.

Step 9. Carefully lift the sections off with forceps. Use probe and scalpel to separate the sections from adhering muscle.

Step 10. Use forceps and scissors to remove all muscles surrounding the organs. Muscles look like small brown strands of twine. Use hand lens and pen flashlight to prevent damage to organs as you probe and cut.

Step 11. Move reproductive gland aside with probe to see stomach, gastric pouches and excretory tubules.

Step 12. To see ganglia and double nerve trunk, raise entire digestive system by sliding probe under it and pressing gently upward. Nerve trunk is on midline resting on ventral exoskeleton. Pick away muscles with forceps to expose nerve trunk.

Step 13. With scissors remove exoskeleton and underlying muscles from top of head between eyes and up to antennae. (Do not cut off the head.) This will expose the "brain."

Fig. 30. Removing Exoskeleton to Expose Internal Organs.

the removal of the legs and wings. This will make it more convenient to handle the body of the specimen as we proceed further. Identify with hand lens the *femur, tibia* and *tarsus* after you remove the legs. Put wings aside for future study. Let's continue by dissecting the male and the female grasshopper as shown in Fig. 29.

Before removing the mouth parts, trace each part back to its point of attachment. (See Fig. 28.) Then lift the part with forceps and, using sharp scissors or scalpel, cut each part away at the point of attachment. Begin by removing each *palpus*. Then remove upper lip and jaws (*mandibles*). Finally, remove the tongue (*hypopharynx*) which is beneath the upper lip. To see points of attachment clearly, use your hand lens.

On a piece of paper, arrange the mouth parts that you removed so that they are in the same position they were in, originally, in the grasshopper's head. This will enable you to see how the grasshopper grasps its food and moves it toward its jaws. Note that the grasshopper chews sideways or laterally. How does this compare with most animals?

Removing the Antenna, Compound Eye and Pronotum

To remove each antenna, cut with scissors at point of attachment to head. Note joints in the antenna. This is what enables it to move and explore the environment. The antennae have nerve endings sensitive to touch and smell. How does this help the grasshopper to explore its environment? Review Fig. 25 and note differences in appendages of crayfish and of grasshopper.

Use a thin, sharp scalpel to dissect out one compound eye. Cut inwardly along the outline of the eye until the eye is free, and remove it. Note blood vessel and nerve connections extending from the eye. Examine the three *ocelli* or simple eyes with a hand lens. Compare these with the compound eyes. What do you see?

To remove the *pronotum* (outer shield) use forceps and scalpel as shown in Fig. 29.

To remove the exoskeleton of abdomen and head, follow the directions in Figs. 29 and 30.

Internal Anatomy of the Grasshopper

It was necessary to remove the appendages and part of the exoskeleton before attempting to examine the internal organs. Study Fig. 31 to identify the main internal organs.

The circulatory system (Fig. 31) is very simple. There is one main vessel that runs along the dorsal midline of the body. Examine the underside of the removed exoskeleton to find the dorsal blood vessel, since it will probably remain attached to the upper part of the abdominal skeleton. The front end of the vessel going to the head is called the dorsal *aorta*. The back part of the vessel has several swellings called hearts. Each swelling (heart) has a tiny opening *(ostium)* equipped with valves which allow blood to enter the heart. When the heart

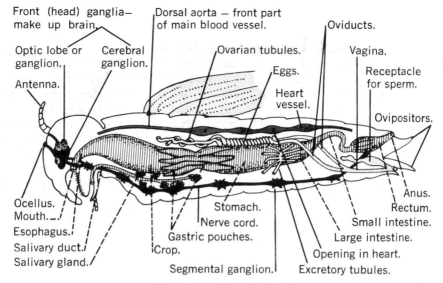

Front (head) ganglia— make up brain.

Optic lobe or ganglion.

Cerebral ganglion.

Antenna.

Dorsal aorta — front part of main blood vessel.

Ovarian tubules.

Eggs.

Heart vessel.

Oviducts.

Vagina.

Receptacle for sperm.

Ovipositors.

Anus.

Rectum.

Small intestine.

Large intestine.

Opening in heart.

Excretory tubules.

Ocellus.

Mouth.

Esophagus.

Salivary duct.

Salivary gland.

Stomach.

Nerve cord.

Gastric pouches.

Crop.

Segmental ganglion.

Fig. 31. Internal Anatomy of Female Grasshopper.

contracts, the valves close and the blood is driven through the vessel toward the head. There the blood passes into a body cavity *(haemocoel)* which is continuous throughout the whole animal. The blood carries digested food which the surrounding cells absorb. Unlike most animals, however, the blood of the grasshopper has little to do with carrying oxygen. It is interesting to note that the grasshopper has no red blood corpuscles. It does have white blood corpuscles. The blood returns from the haemocoel to the *ostia* (plural of ostium) of the hearts and follows the circulatory route all over again. This type of circulatory system is called an *open system* because the blood flows freely through open tissue spaces. Unlike the grasshopper, man has a closed circulatory system in which the blood is always contained in blood vessels.

Find the dorsal aorta and the hearts in Fig. 31. Then examine the upper part of the exposed specimen with a hand lens and locate the dorsal aorta and the hearts. If you do not see the hearts on the specimen, look at the exoskeleton you have cut away. Use a hand lens to see the ostium or pore in each heart.

Respiratory System of the Grasshopper

The grasshopper has no gills and no lungs. How then

Abdominal air sacs — oxygen enters blood directly from air sacs. (No blood vessels are present.)

Large air sac in thorax.

Connects with air sacs and tracheal tubes in head.

Dorsal trunk.

Lateral trunk.

Ventral trunk.

Spiracles — air enters first 4 spiracles in abdomen and leaves through last 6 spiracles.

View of first 4 segments of abdomen. Other organs omitted for the sake of simplification.

Fig. 32. System of Air Tubes (Tracheal Tubes) in Grasshopper.

does it breathe? Look first at Fig. 27 and find the spiracles. Now find them on your dissected specimen. You will probably have to dissect another specimen to study the respiratory system because it is usually damaged during dissection unless great care is exercised. Place the narrow tip of the medicine dropper or the needle tip of a hypodermic syringe firmly against the opening of a spiracle. Squeeze the rubber bulb gently. Hold a hand lens over the side of the abdomen and observe the slight strain or swelling on a sac-like structure called the abdominal air sac (see Fig. 32). This may not work with the first spiracle because the spiracular valve may be closed. If so, try another spiracle. When the grasshopper breathes in, the valves in the first four pairs of spiracles are open and the valves in the last six pairs of spiracles are closed. The abdomen works like a bellows. As it expands and contracts, the valves of the spiracles take turns opening and closing. Thus fresh air moves in and used air moves out. The faster the grasshopper moves the faster the air circulates through the body.

With Fig. 32 as a guide use a good light and a hand lens or micro dissecting microscope to locate the main parts of the respiratory system on your specimen. With scissors cut a small section of a *tracheal* (air) tube ⅛ of an inch long and examine under low power microscope (50x to 100x). Notice the spiral rings that hold the tubes open at all times. The oxygen taken in through the spiracles quickly reaches all the cells in the body. Farmers take advantage of this type of respiratory system in the grasshopper by using *aerosol* (air sprayed) insecticides. The insecticides are taken in quickly through the spiracles and the tracheal tubes. Thus the poisons used to kill grasshoppers work rapidly.

Digestive System of the Grasshopper

A study of the bottom of Fig. 31 will show the arrangement of the parts of the digestive system. Notice that all the labels related to the digestive system are indicated by broken lines to help you identify the parts in your specimen. The digestive system of the grasshopper is somewhat like that of the crayfish and the earthworm. The digestive organs are easy to find. (See Fig. 31.) However, it may be necessary, if the specimen is a female, to move the eggs aside in order to see the entire stomach, small intestine and rectum. Locate the following digestive organs in the specimen:

Mouth—located behind the mandibles. Use your hand lens and a probe to find it.

Salivary glands—located on each side ventrally in the thorax. They send their secretion of saliva into the mouth region through the salivary ducts.

Gullet—a short tube leading from the mouth to the crop.

Crop—a large, thin-walled storage organ that connects with the stomach.

Gastric pouches—several large digestive glands that secrete digestive juices into the stomach.

Stomach—a large chamber in which food is digested.

Large intestine—a short, wide tube that connects the stomach with the small intestine. It conducts wastes into the small intestine.

Small intestine—a short, narrow, coiled tube that carries wastes into the rectum.

Rectum—a chamber shaped like an inflated football that stores wastes temporarily and eventually forces the wastes out through the anus.

Anus—opening at the end of the digestive tract to the outside of the body.

Excretory System of the Grasshopper

There are a number of *tubules* at the juncture between

the stomach and large intestine. The outer end of each tubule opens into the body cavity and takes in liquid wastes. The wastes are carried by the tubules into the large intestine and ultimately out through the anus.

Reproductive System of the Grasshopper

Fig. 31 shows the internal anatomy of the female grasshopper. The anatomy of the male and the female grasshopper is essentially the same. The main external differences are that the female has a pointed abdomen, forked at the tip, while the male's abdomen is rounded at the tip and not forked. (See Figs. 27 and 29.) Internally, the reproductive organs are different.

In the female grasshopper a pair of ovarian tubules (small, coiled tubes) located above the gastric pouches, produce eggs which are arranged dorsally like a row of pennies on end. These tubules connect with a pair of oviducts that separate to branch over the large intestine. The branches meet below the rectum and below the nerve cord to form a canal called the *vagina*. Just above the vagina is a small sac, a sperm receptacle, which stores the sperm cells after mating until the eggs are laid, at which time the eggs and sperm meet. The grasshopper uses its ovipositors (See Fig. 31) to force its abdomen into the earth where it forms a burrow. The fertilized eggs are neatly laid in the burrow. There they develop into the young grasshoppers called *nymphs*. When the young grasshoppers are sufficiently developed they emerge from their burrows and start foraging for their meals.

The male grasshopper has two *testes* which produce sperm cells. The sperm leave each testis through a tube called the *vas deferens*. The tubes leading from the testes unite to form a duct into which glands secrete a fluid. The sperm cells swim in this fluid during mating with the female. An extension of the duct formed by the testes transfers the sperm from the male into the female. If you want to locate these parts, dissect the male grasshopper, using the same dissecting technique as you used for the female grasshopper.

Nervous System of the Grasshopper

The nervous system of the grasshopper is quite similar to the nervous system of the crayfish. The heads of each have

52

large *ganglia* which may be called the brain. In the grasshopper, as in the earthworm, the ganglia are ventrally located, segmentally arranged and connected by a double nerve cord. This is very clearly seen in the grasshopper. Using fine scissors, expose the brain by cutting away the muscles and connective tissue that surround it. Locate the nerve trunk and several of the segmental ganglia.

Now that we have explored the anatomy of the preserved grasshopper, let's try some challenging experiments with live grasshoppers.

Project 1: Fountain of Youth

Why does an insect larva like the caterpillar grow to its full size before it begins the remarkable changes that result in the adult butterfly or moth? One important reason has already been discovered. Part of the larva's brain produces a chemical known as juvenile hormone. As long as this hormone is produced, the larva remains a larva. It does not undergo change or metamorphosis until the hormone secretion stops. Then the larva develops into the adult.

How would you like to try to produce a giant larva or a giant adult insect? It has been done! Several scientists have succeeded in producing giant moths. Let's see if the same experiment will produce giant grasshoppers. To try this you will need the following:

Several live, young grasshoppers: you can keep them in jars filled with twigs and leaves, covered with perforated screw jar covers. The young grasshopper, unlike the young moth or butterfly, looks like the adult.

Five to ten abdomens of adult male moths: moths may be used even if they are old and dried up, because the hormone in the abdomen remains unspoiled indefinitely.

A mortar and pestle for grinding the abdomens, a tablespoon of clean building sand (obtainable at hardware stores) to mix with the abdomens as you grind them and about 25 ml (milliliters) of diethyl ether to mix with the ground up abdomens. *This chemical should be used in school under the supervision of a science teacher. It must be used in a well ventilated room, away from an open flame.*

A centrifuge and 2 centrifuge tubes: the centrifuge is a machine that whirls 2 or more special centrifuge test tubes

Step 1. Fold filter paper into quarters as shown here.

Filter paper.

Funnel.

Step 2. Open paper to form cone with one quarter segment separated from the others and inserted into funnel.

Step 3. Insert funnel into vial.

Fig. 33. How to Make a Filter.

around at high speed. When a mixture in these tubes is centrifuged, the heavier materials in the mixture go to the bottom of the tubes and the lighter materials rise toward the top. This helps us to separate the constituents of a mixture. *This too should be done only in school under the supervision of a science teacher.*

A small glass funnel, round filter paper, 2 or 3 glass vials with screw tops (20 to 30 ml in size), a half pound of non-absorbent cotton, a 50 ml beaker, a glass stirring rod and a fine artist's paint brush.

Begin your experiment by placing the moth abdomens in the mortar. Add ½ teaspoon of sand and grind the abdomens with the pestle until the mixture is like a powder. Now continue as follows:

Step 1. Transfer the mixture to the beaker and add enough ether to reach a level of about 1 inch in the beaker. Stir with the glass rod, gently but thoroughly; then pour equal amounts of the mixture into 2 centrifuge tubes to a level of ½ inch from the top of each tube. Now centrifuge the tubes for 10 minutes.

Step 2. Fold filter paper as shown in Fig. 33, and place into

54

mouth of funnel as shown. Press filter paper against moistened funnel and insert tube of funnel into one of the vials.

Step 3. Pour liquid from centrifuge tubes on filter paper in funnel. Wait until all the liquid comes through the filter paper into the vial. Stopper the vial with cotton, firmly but not tightly.

Step 4. Place stoppered vial near open window to hasten evaporation of ether. The hormone will appear as a golden colored liquid.

Step 5. Dip the paint brush into the hormone and paint a thin stripe on the abdomen of one of the young grasshoppers, but do not cover the spiracles. Keep an untreated grasshopper in a separate container as a control, for comparison. Add several leaves to each container. Keep accurate records of size and other visible changes. Now wait for results! Try this same experiment with other insects. Sooner or later the results will prove exciting.

Project 2: How Powerful Are a Grasshopper's Leg Muscles?

Recent scientific experiments have shown that a grasshopper can jump 20 times its own length. If a human five feet tall could do that he could jump a distance of 100 feet, or half an average city block. The grasshopper can jump 10 times its body length straight up in the air. Imagine a boy five feet tall jumping 50 feet high, the height of a four or five story building! Clearly, the grasshopper has powerful leg muscles. Can we measure this power? Yes. We can use simplified techniques similar to those used by G. Hoyle, a zoologist, in his studies of the grasshopper. He used electric stimulation on the *anal cerci* of the grasshopper to cause it to raise its legs (see Fig. 34). Weights were tied to the legs and he was able to measure the weight that the grasshopper's legs could lift.

Let us try to measure the power of a grasshopper's legs with the use of an *inductorium*, a device consisting of electromagnets that is capable of producing small electric shocks when connected to one 1.5-volt or two 1.5-volt dry cell batteries (see Fig. 34). There are inexpensive inductoriums sold by scientific supply houses.

On each side of the abdominal tip of the grasshopper are tiny structures called *anal cerci*. The anal cerci are sense organs that transmit impulses along the nerve fibers to the nerve centers that control the leg muscles of the grasshopper.

The brain is also stimulated by the transmission of impulses from the anal cerci, and relays impulses back to the legs. When these cerci are touched several times quickly with the wire ends of the inductorium the grasshopper responds by flexing its legs to leap. It is the strength of the flexing that we will measure.

Using cotton thread, tie a standard weight of 1/10 grams to the *tarsus* or toe of the grasshopper. Then touch the cerci rapidly with the exposed ends of the wires from the inductorium. The legs will flex and raise the weight. Repeat the process with heavier weights, using a different grasshopper

Fig. 34. Set-up for Measuring Lifting Power of Grasshopper's Legs.

Step 1. Remove insulation from ends of 5 pieces of bell wire and connect to batteries and inductorium as shown.

Step 2. Place a 4" x ½" square of plasticine (modelling clay) on a block of wood, same size. With a pencil press down and form a groove in the plasticine about the size and depth of a grasshopper.

Step 3. Place live grasshopper in groove, turned on its back, its legs sticking up. Gently work the plasticine over its body with your fingers until only the head, legs and the tip of the abdomen along the spiracles remain exposed as shown.

Inductorium.

Inductorium's terminals

Dial controlling current.

Electrodes (wires) delivering shock by electrical stimulus.

Terminals for connection with dry cells.

Tarsus (toe).

Anal cerci.

Weight.

1.5 volt batteries.

Wood block.

Plasticine (modelling clay).

tor each test, since the tested grasshopper may be injured during the test. Determine finally how much weight a grasshopper will lift.

Weigh the grasshopper on a balance scale in your school laboratory. Compare its weight with the weight its leg can lift. How much weight can the average man lift in comparison with his own weight?

Project 3: Veins Will Tell

Collect different species of grasshoppers and other members of the group (such as locust) called the *Orthoptera* to which the grasshoppers belong. Detach their wings and make closeup photographs to show the arrangement of the veins in the wings. Assign a number to each of the main veins and to each of the large branches of the main veins. Arrange the wings and the photographs in a series, with the wings showing the most similar vein arrangement closest, those slightly different, next in line and so on. You will find that a knowledge of the arrangement of wing veins can help you to distinguish insects and their relatives. Your "vein print" technique might compare with finger printing as a means of identification.

We have examined the anatomy of an insect, the grasshopper. It is exciting to realize how one animal is related to another by understanding how their structures compare with one another. Thus we can see that despite the great differences between the earthworm and the grasshopper there are important fundamental likenesses that reveal distant descent.

We have also investigated possible lines of exploration that have recently been started by scientists. These are only suggested beacons that can light the way to your own paths of experimentation. Now let us move on to a completely different kind of animal, the starfish.

5 Star of the Sea — The Starfish.

THE STARFISH is not a fish. It has no internal skeleton like that of a fish or other vertebrates. Why then should we be interested in dissecting the starfish? Scientists believe that some member of the starfish family became the ancestor of the backboned animals, the vertebrates, many millions of years ago. It is fascinating to see how different they are from vertebrate animals.

The starfish is an enemy of man. It can destroy huge beds of oysters which are an important food source for man. The starfish eats oysters in a curious way. First it settles its rays or arms around the shell of a living oyster. Then it starts a tug-of-war, the oyster using its muscles to keep the shell tightly closed, while the starfish tries to force the shell open. The struggle is uneven. The oyster depends entirely on its muscles which sooner or later tire. The starfish uses the power of the sea (described on page 62) and it never tires. As the oyster's shell finally opens, the starfish causes its stomach to move out of its body and around the flesh of the victim. The starfish then secretes digestive juices from the digestive glands in the rays, and dinner is over. The starfish takes in little waste material from the food it eats because the food is digested externally and, as can be expected, it has a poorly developed intestine and rectum.

The most important weapon of a scientist is knowledge. It was knowledge of the structure and habits of the starfish that made it possible to cut down the size of the starfish population and thus save the oyster industry. For many years oystermen used to catch and smash starfish and throw the pieces back into the sea. But they discovered that this practice almost ruined the oyster industry because starfish have

Fig. 35. Starfish—Topside.　　　**Fig. 36. Underside of Starfish.**
Courtesy Carolina Biological Supply Company.

the power of regeneration, or regrowth. Many of the rays that were pitched back into the sea grew into whole new starfish, thereby further endangering the oyster beds. Research led to the present methods of using sea mops—mops made of cloth or string that are dragged along the sea bottom to catch the starfish, which are then left in the sun to dry and to die. They can also be killed in hot water tanks,or by exposure to live steam.

Preparing for Dissection of the Starfish

For dissecting purposes obtain an injected specimen of *Asterias forbesi* or *Asterias rubens*. Use the same basic equipment as you used for the earthworm dissection. In addition, you will need a pair of sharp, pointed, strong scissors about 4 inches long, a hand magnifying lens with a diameter of one inch or more and about 5x magnification, and a glass microscope slide. A low power microscope (20x to 50x) would be helpful.

Fig. 37 will be your guide to dissecting the starfish. Because each arm, or ray, is like the other rays on both the outside and inside, we can dissect one arm to see the digestive organs, another arm to see the reproductive organs and so on. Fig. 37 is arranged in 7 parts, marked A to G. Each part shows where to dissect and shows views of the different internal organs. Your dissected starfish should look like Fig. 37 when you have completed the dissection.

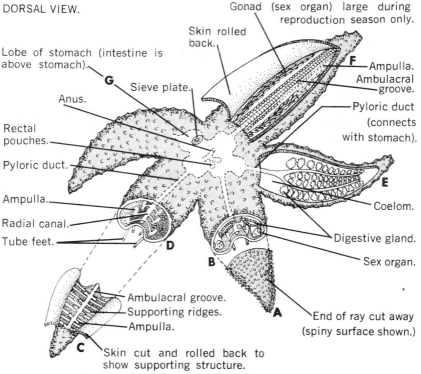

DORSAL VIEW.

Gonad (sex organ) large during reproduction season only.

Skin rolled back.

Lobe of stomach (intestine is above stomach).

G Sieve plate.

Anus.

Rectal pouches.

Pyloric duct.

Ampulla.

Radial canal.

Tube feet.

F Ampulla.
Ambulacral groove.

Pyloric duct (connects with stomach).

E

Coelom.

Digestive gland.

Sex organ.

D

B

A

Ambulacral groove.
Supporting ridges.
Ampulla.

C Skin cut and rolled back to show supporting structure.

End of ray cut away (spiny surface shown.)

Fig. 37. Dissection of Starfish—External and Internal Anatomy.

External Anatomy

Before dissecting the starfish, let us examine the external characteristics. Place your specimen in the dissecting pan with dorsal side up. The dorsal side has no grooves or tube feet. (See Fig. 35.)

Locate the five rays, or arms. (Specimens may have four rays or even fewer, if rays have been broken off prior to handling. In rare instances, starfish have been found with up to 25 rays.) Now look for the very small circular disc located near the starfish's center. Note that it is slightly off center. This is the *sieve plate*. (See Figs. 35 and 37.) The sieve plate is a perforated disc through which water enters the body of the starfish.

With the paint brush used in the grasshopper experiment or with a piece of cheese cloth wrapped around your finger, stroke the skin on each ray. Note its spiny nature. Examine the skin with the hand lens to see the spines in closer detail.

Turn the specimen ventral side up. With Fig. 37 as a guide, examine the tube feet (part D) with the hand lens. Find the mouth in the center of the specimen (see Fig. 36). Notice the groove that runs from the tip of each ray toward the center of the starfish (see Fig. 36). The tube feet are arranged on each side of the groove (part D of Fig. 37).

Internal Anatomy

Let us begin the dissection as shown in part A. Cut off about one inch from the end of one ray. Force the sharp pointed end of the scissors through the skin at the side of the ray. Then cut the skin around the ray in a ring. Move the skin slightly to one side and snip off the end of the ray.

Examine the cut end of the ray at part B with your hand lens. Note the feathery looking digestive glands and, under them, the sex organs near the beginning of the ray where they join the central part of the body.

To understand something about the framework of the ray, cut off the end of another ray as shown in part C. Cut it off in the same way as in part A. Then, using forceps, clean out the digestive organ and sex organs, if present. (If sex organs are not at peak of development they will not extend as far as the last inch of the ray.) Now cut the skin with scissors and roll it back, as shown in part C. Locate the structures labeled in part C. Examine the inside wall of the ray with the hand lens. You will see the supporting ridges, the bulb-like *ampullae* (tiny sacs that are part of the tube feet described in Fig. 38) and tiny openings in inner wall. These openings are pores that connect with the projecting gill tube and are part of the external gills which help the starfish to breathe.

Cut off a strip of skin about ¼ inch wide from the loose flap shown in part C. Place the piece of skin on the glass slide with the spines pointing upward. Examine with the hand lens or with the low power microscope, if available. Identify the following structures in the skin:

Large, stiff spines used for protection and to provide friction for gripping the sea bottom, sand, rocks and other objects.

Small hair-like gills used by the starfish to take in oxygen.

Tiny pincers called *pedicellaria* that look like pliers. They are used to grip minute objects and to clean the skin of the starfish. The pedicellaria and the spines combine to doom the

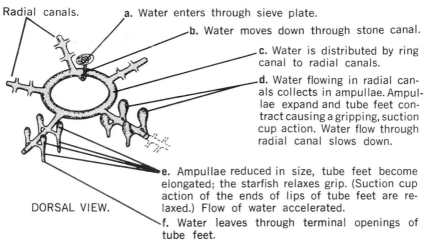

Radial canals.

a. Water enters through sieve plate.

b. Water moves down through stone canal.

c. Water is distributed by ring canal to radial canals.

d. Water flowing in radial canals collects in ampullae. Ampullae expand and tube feet contract causing a gripping, suction cup action. Water flow through radial canal slows down.

e. Ampullae reduced in size, tube feet become elongated; the starfish relaxes grip. (Suction cup action of the ends of lips of tube feet are relaxed.) Flow of water accelerated.

f. Water leaves through terminal openings of tube feet.

DORSAL VIEW.

Fig. 38. Action of Tube Feet of Starfish.

starfish when oystermen use their sea mops to clear the starfish from the oyster beds. These structures attach themselves to the sea mops and thus the starfish are removed from the sea to perish on land.

Transportation by Tube Feet

To enable you to identify better the water transport, or water vascular system which helps the starfish move about, the digestive gland and the sex organs have been omitted in part D of Fig. 37. Raise the digestive gland of the specimen with a probe or with forceps and find the structures labeled in part D. Count the number of tube feet on one inch of skin. How many inches are there in all five rays of your starfish? Measure the length of one ray. Multiply this length by five, the usual number of rays on the starfish. Now estimate the total number of tube feet on the rays of the starfish by multiplying the number of tube feet on one inch by the combined length of all the rays. Does this help you to understand one reason why the starfish can force open the shell of a resisting oyster?

The starfish has a simple, primitive nervous system without a brain. But it does have a highly developed method of locomotion resulting from the action of its tube feet, the special structures that are connected to a system of canals (see Fig. 38). Most animals draw their power from the action of their muscles. While the starfish has muscles, its main source of power is the sea. It uses the water of the sea to create a form of suction at the ends of its tube feet. This suction enables the starfish to move and to grasp objects. As some of the tube feet hold on to the sea bottom, others release their hold. The free part of the starfish then contracts by means of its muscles and moves toward the part that is holding to the sea bottom. The rear tube feet then take hold and the front ones are released. In this way the starfish "pulls" itself along. As long as there is water the starfish has power.

Digestive System of the Starfish

The digestive system of the starfish is made up of the following parts:

Mouth—a small opening in the center of its lower or ventral side.

Stomach—a lobed, muscular sac shown by the dotted lines in part G. Each lobe, or section of the stomach has a tube called the *pyloric duct* that connects with the digestive gland in each ray.

To expose the digestive gland and pyloric duct in one ray, cut a section of the skin away as shown on part E. Using scissors, start the cut near the tip of the ray along one side. Then cut in a straight line toward the center of the starfish. Do the same along the other side and cut the skin off where the ray meets the center of the body. The digestive gland is now exposed. Raise the digestive gland gently with a probe and trace its connection to the pyloric duct. Examine the digestive gland with a hand lens to see the many tiny structures that secrete the digestive juice.

Intestine—a thin sac just above the stomach (see part G) in which some digestion takes place and wastes are moved toward the rectal pouches and the anus.

Rectal pouches—two very small sacs that store small amounts of wastes temporarily. Little is actually known about these structures.

Anus—a very short tube coming from the intestine, and opening to the outside through the upper or dorsal part of the starfish. Wastes are discharged through the anus.

The Reproductive System

To study the reproductive organs (part F, Fig. 37) cut open another ray in almost the same way as described in part E of Fig. 37. First lift with forceps the exposed digestive gland

and cut the pyloric duct close to the place where it joins the stomach. Now remove the entire digestive gland. This will enable you to more easily expose the *gonads* (reproductive organs) which are below the digestive gland and on each side of the pyloric duct.

During the breeding season the reproductive organs enlarge until they almost fill the entire ray, but at other times they will be small. You will probably get starfish with small gonads because the supply houses generally do not collect starfish during the breeding season. The starfish bodies are so crowded with eggs in the breeding season that other organs are hard to see. Moreover, the starfish are easily damaged at that time and are hard to preserve.

The testes of the male starfish discharge sperm and the ovaries of the female starfish discharge eggs into the water during the breeding season. The sperm and eggs join together and the unions develop into bilaterally symmetrical larvae which develop into adult starfish. Although both the testes and the ovaries look alike, page 67 describes how to tell them apart.

Locating the Digestive System

To expose the stomach, intestine, rectal glands and anus of the starfish, carefully study part G of Fig. 37 before dissecting. (This area is, of course, covered by the starfish's spiny surface.) Note that the dotted lines form the outline of the stomach. Remember that the intestine is *above* the stomach and very close to the skin. With these two facts in mind, cut, with scissors, a circle of skin about 1½ inches in diameter from the top center of the starfish and remove it. Make the cut as shallow as you can. Even then, the intestine will probably be damaged. Be careful not to disturb the *sieve plate* and the *stone canal*, the tube that leads down from the sieve plate (see Fig. 38). Locate the stomach and the other labeled structures in that area. Push a probe downward through the stomach. It should pass through the gullet and out through the mouth without meeting any obstruction.

Try to trace the stone canal to its connection with the ring canal (see Fig. 38 for details). Use forceps to pick away tissue from the canals. This operation is difficult. If you succeed in doing this neatly you may have the makings of a fine surgeon!

A Heartless, Bloodless Circulatory System

The dissection of the starfish has shown you that the starfish is very different from the crayfish or the grasshopper and their cousins, and that the starfish is really a very simple kind of organism as compared with the crayfish and the insects. It has no heart or blood vessels, and circulation is accomplished mostly by water flowing through the open body cavity or *coelom*. Sea water is its blood and the open, continuous spaces in its body substitute for blood vessels. Water enters through the gills in the skin and moves into the body cavity (coelom). There it is forced to circulate by cells with little projections that lash the water as the starfish adventures on the ocean bottom. The starfish has small *amoeboid* cells—cells that can change their shape. These behave very much like certain types of white blood corpuscles in our blood.

Yet, in spite of his many anatomical omissions, this interesting little fellow and his family contributed a larval ancestor that gave rise to the highest group of animal life, the vertebrates. Read about the *bipinnaria larva* of the starfish and the theoretical larva, the *dipleurula*. It will help you to understand better the links between the invertebrates and the vertebrates. Compare this larva with *tornaria* larva of the higher group of animals. The resemblance emphasizes evolutionary linkage.

There are many projects that are begun simply because we become interested in an idea. Often such projects result in the development of very satisfying lifelong hobbies that provide color, interest, drama and many opportunities for scientific research for science-oriented people. Following are several projects that may enrich your life for many years to come.

Project 1: Ocean Life in Your Home

Many people keep a fresh water aquarium stocked with tropical fish in their living rooms. Maintaining such aquaria is an interesting hobby which serves as a conversation piece and as a source of living beauty. Few people know that a marine aquarium can be maintained in the home and can be even more attractive and exciting than a fresh water aquarium.

You do not have to live near the sea to have a marine aquarium. Small chemical packets may be purchased from biological supply houses which, dissolved in fresh water, produce artificial sea water in which marine life can flourish. Directions for the use of the chemicals and for the care of the aquarium are provided by the suppliers. However, experience has shown that some natural sea water is desirable if the animals are to survive for extended periods of time. A satisfactory ratio is about one gallon of natural sea water to nine gallons of artificial sea water. A one to ten mixture will do the job as well. There are several things you have to be careful to do when you set up a marine aquarium:

Use an all glass tank or a tank where no metal will come in contact with the water. (Metal reacts to salts in "sea" water and produces compounds poisonous to fish.) Handle the animals with a plastic salad spoon and fork combination. Do not touch the animals with anything made of metal.

Keep the tank away from strong light or direct sunlight which can be injurious to the fish. Use fluorescent lighting. Hobby shops sell tanks equipped with fluorescent lighting.

Use clean beach sand only. No other kind of sand is satisfactory. The sand can be purchased if necessary. Include plants like sea lettuce and cladophora. They are good oxygen producers.

Aerate the water continuously with an aquarium pump which drives air into the water.

Use two tanks, a large tank (about 10 gallon size) and a small tank (about 2 gallon size). The small tank is used for feeding the animals, and since the fish are kept there for a ½ hour or less ordinarily, it does not need any lighting or any of the other trimmings.

Keep the main tank near a cold window. Keep the window open at the bottom about 2 inches if possible. Try to hold the temperature of the water below 60 degrees Fahrenheit. The temperature may be kept down during the warm months by adding to the water in the tank, daily, a tray full of ice cubes from a rubber or plastic tray. (No metal ions will be transfered into the tank if ice from a rubber or plastic tray is used.)

Do not crowd the tank. About 6 to 10 small animals are all that a 10 gallon tank can maintain. You can use such creatures as starfish, sea urchin, clam, sea snail, barnacle, very small fish, scallop, sponge and jellyfish.

Feed the animals sparingly.

It is especially interesting to change the scene every so

often by discarding old stock—exchange with friends or provide "decent burial"—and experimenting with different combinations of animals. Note how they react to each other. Some get along with each other, some are indifferent to their neighbors while others do something about their "grievances."

Project 2:   Is It a He or a She?

The male and female sex organs of the starfish look alike. How can we be sure which one is which? This can best be done with fresh starfish which you may be able to collect or get from a fishing boat. If that is not possible for you then preserved specimens will have to do.

Dissect an arm of the starfish as shown in part F of Fig. 37. Locate the sex organs and remove a tiny piece of tissue from the sex organ with forceps. Place the tissue sample on a microscope slide. Add a drop of water to the tissue. Then spread or tease the tissue with two dissecting needles. Place a cover slip over the thinned out tissue and examine it with a microscope, first under low power and then under high power (400x or higher). The male organs, testes, will show minute cells that have a tiny tail or flagellum. These cells are the sperm cells. The female organs, ovaries, will show cells that look like tiny pearls. These cells are the egg cells. They are much larger than the sperm cells.

Project 3:   "Disappearing" Through Camouflage

Obtain several small, live flounder (about 2 inches in length). Keep them in a marine aquarium (see Project 1). Use a second, smaller all glass tank (2 gallon size) for the following experiment:

Place colored paper around the bottom and three sides of the tank. Transfer the flounder to the small tank for two to four hours. Observe the color changes that take place. This may help answer the question: Why is a flounder so hard to see in its natural surroundings? Change the color patterns every two or three days. Record the effect of these changes on the skin color of the flounder. Can you tell what the advantages of these color changes are to the flounder? Some fascinating work has been pioneered in this field.

6 The Squid — The Hunter and the Hunted.

THE SEA has spawned and nurtured many strange creatures, from invisible forms to leviathans of the sea, from plankton to Moby Dick. Among the most unusual and interesting of these is the squid. For centuries the name squid has meant many things to many people. The fisherman thinks of squid as bait; others see squid as food. Many sailors have dreaded the squid as the legendary Giant Sea-Devil or Haf-gufa. Imagine yourself in a longboat idly gazing at the ocean swells, perhaps even trailing your hand over the gunwhales, when suddenly the water parts, revealing "what looks at first like a number of islands surrounded by something that floats and fluctuates like seaweed. At last several bright horns rise as high as the masts of good-sized vessels. It is said that if the arms were to lay hold of the largest man-of-war they would pull it down to the bottom." This description was written in 1751 in the book, *Natural History of Norway*. Is it any wonder that the squid excites the imagination?

The giant squid is 10 to 15 feet long and has tentacles 30 to 40 feet long. It is rarely seen alive because it inhabits deep waters, but whalers have seen it often in the stomachs of killed whales. The digested squid becomes a greenish gristle with a strange fragrance. This is the fabulous ambergris used in making expensive perfumes.

Of course, not all squid are giants. There are different species. The *Loligo pealii* is probably the most common type of squid in the temperate waters of the Atlantic Ocean. Fishermen who have used this type of squid as bait are little impressed with the ghastly hue of the dead squid. But when seen alive, its beauty of form and color is striking. Disturb it and the colors change rapidly, seeming to flow from one shade

Fig. 39. The Squid (Loligo pealii).
Courtesy Marine Studios, Marineland, Florida.

to another. To escape its enemies, the squid sometimes seems to disappear behind a black cloud which is formed as it discharges the contents of its *ink sac*.

Legend has it that squid are moongazers. They will swim toward the light of the moon reflected by the ocean and often run aground. Perhaps that is only legend. But it is a fact that fishermen often catch squid by lighting fires on a beach or by hanging a lamp on the prow of a skiff and rowing backwards towards land. The squid follow the firelight or lamplight and become stranded at the shore.

To biologists and other scientists the squid is remarkable in other ways. Together with its close relative, the octopus, the squid is among the most specialized of all invertebrate animals. It has no segments and no exoskeleton, yet it is part of the same species which include clams, snails and oysters, all of which do have a shell or exoskeleton. In fact, the squid is more unusual because its body plan is so different from other animals. In most animals it is easy to determine what side is dorsal or ventral and what part is anterior or posterior. In the squid these regions are difficult to identify. To understand this, look at a snail, a relative of the squid. Fig. 40 shows the outline of a snail moving up a glass side of an aquarium. Imagine that you could take hold of the snail at point V and point D

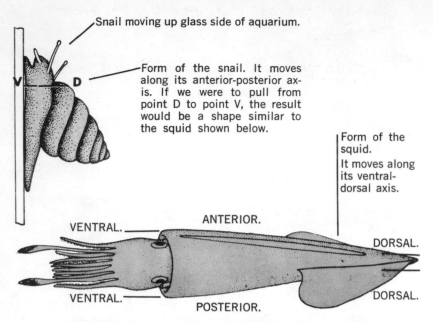

Snail moving up glass side of aquarium.

Form of the snail. It moves along its anterior-posterior axis. If we were to pull from point D to point V, the result would be a shape similar to the squid shown below.

Form of the squid.
It moves along its ventral-dorsal axis.

VENTRAL.

ANTERIOR.

DORSAL.

VENTRAL.

POSTERIOR.

DORSAL.

Fig. 40. Comparing Form of a Snail With Form of a Squid.

and just pull the snail from these points in opposite directions in a straight line. The animal would elongate between V and D and become slender. The result would closely resemble the squid in Fig. 40. Actually no one stretched a snail to make a squid. The curious shape, in which the head became the ventral part of the body instead of the anterior part, as in most animals, was evolved by the ancestors of the squid.

The squid may be called the rocket of the sea. Hold it upright and it looks like a rocket resting on its launching platform. It moves by means of jet propulsion, a principle which man has only recently mastered and is now using in missiles, rockets, planes and small boats. By examining the anatomy of the squid we can understand how it uses the jet stream for locomotion.

External Anatomy—Identifying Structures

To dissect the squid, obtain an injected specimen, the *Loligo pealii*, about 10 inches long. Use the equipment recommended for the dissection of the earthworm.

To study the external anatomy of the squid, place the squid on the dissecting pan. Locate the structures labeled in

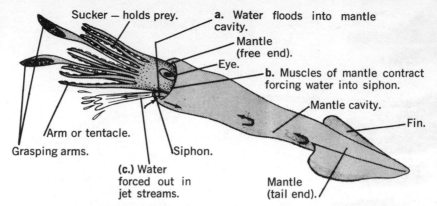

Sucker — holds prey.

a. Water floods into mantle cavity.

Mantle (free end).

Eye.

b. Muscles of mantle contract forcing water into siphon.

Mantle cavity.

Fin.

Arm or tentacle.

Grasping arms.

Siphon.

(c.) Water forced out in jet streams.

Mantle (tail end).

Fig. 41. External Anatomy of Squid—Method of Locomotion of Squid Explained.

Fig. 41. Use the hand lens to examine the *suckers* in the tentacles. The suckers are equipped with horny teeth that help to trap the living prey, small fish, crabs and other squid. Yes, the squid is cannibalistic. Note that two of the arms are longer than the others. These are the *grasping arms* that hold the victim and bring it to the squid's mouth. There is a loose edge of tissue near the eyes. This is the open end of the *mantle,* a muscular sac that surrounds all of the body except the head and neck. Locate the *siphon* and observe that it can be moved in any direction.

Internal Anatomy—Dissecting the Squid

Lift the free end of the mantle just above the siphon with a pair of forceps (see Fig. 42). With scissors cut through the mantle in a straight line to the pointed end of the body. Spread the mantle and pin it to the dissecting board as shown in Fig. 43. This exposes the *mantle chamber* and all the internal organs, except those in the head. Locate the supporting cartilages in the free end of the mantle. Trace the siphon backward, using a probe to move aside the muscles that are attached to the siphon and that control it.

At this point we are ready to understand why the squid can move like a rocket. Water is taken into the body through the open edge of the mantle. The muscular mantle then contracts, strongly sealing the body cavity at the neck and forcing a large volume of water through the narrow opening of the siphon. This produces a powerful jet stream (see Fig. 41). The muscles around the siphon contract and cause the siphon to

71

Step 1. Lift free end of mantle with forceps.

Step 2. Cut in straight line to tail end of mantle.

Step 3. Spread and roll back cut ends of mantle. Pin to dissecting pan as shown in Fig. 43.

Fig. 42. Exposing the Internal Organs.

change direction, as determined by impulses from the squid's nervous system. If the siphon points backward the squid darts forward toward its prey, with its arms held close together, until it is ready to strike. If the siphon points forward the squid will dart backward. The siphon then acts as a rudder, as well as a jet. The fins help to stabilize the motion of the squid and also act as rudders. Some squid can swim forward slowly by means of gentle movements of the tentacles and the wave-like motion of the fins.

Digestive System of the Squid

With scissors, cut off the siphon and the muscles attached to it. Then with the scissors make a shallow cut starting at the neck and up through the head, to a point midway between the eyes and slightly past the eyes, until you reach the rounded muscular organ that surrounds the jaws. Observe that the jaws are like the beak of a parrot. They are excellently suited for cutting and tearing. Locate the mouth by pushing the probe between the jaws. Separate the tentacles to see where the probe emerges.

Find the *esophagus*, a narrow tube below the jaws which connects the mouth with the stomach. Trace, with the probe, the path of the esophagus to the stomach as it enters the long, narrow liver at the base of the head. At the front of the liver, just below it, is a salivary gland. This gland produces a digestive juice that is delivered through a duct to the mouth. The esophagus leaves the liver about midway and connects with the stomach after it passes the *pancreas*, a small, white, lobed organ lying below the kidneys.

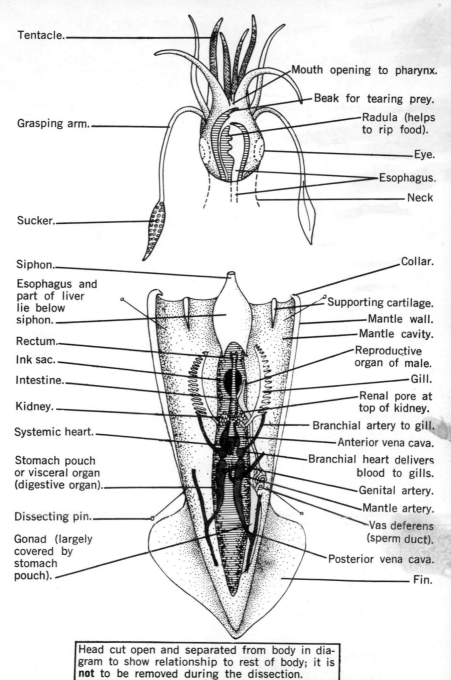

Tentacle.

Mouth opening to pharynx.

Beak for tearing prey.

Grasping arm.

Radula (helps to rip food).

Eye.

Esophagus.

Neck

Sucker.

Siphon.

Collar.

Esophagus and part of liver lie below siphon.

Supporting cartilage.

Mantle wall.

Mantle cavity.

Rectum.

Reproductive organ of male.

Ink sac.

Gill.

Intestine.

Renal pore at top of kidney.

Kidney.

Branchial artery to gill.

Systemic heart.

Anterior vena cava.

Branchial heart delivers blood to gills.

Stomach pouch or visceral organ (digestive organ).

Genital artery.

Mantle artery.

Dissecting pin.

Vas deferens (sperm duct).

Gonad (largely covered by stomach pouch).

Posterior vena cava.

Fin.

Head cut open and separated from body in diagram to show relationship to rest of body; it is **not** to be removed during the dissection.

Fig. 43. Internal Organs of Male Squid—Nervous System Omitted.

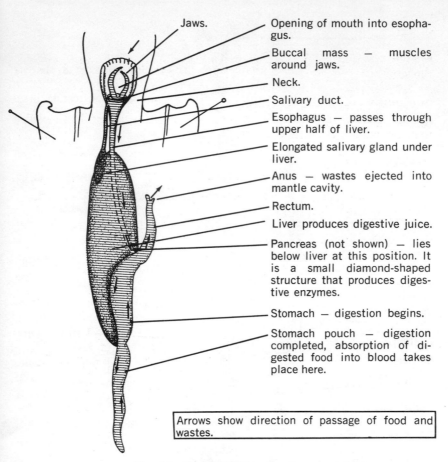

Jaws.

Opening of mouth into esophagus.

Buccal mass — muscles around jaws.

Neck.

Salivary duct.

Esophagus — passes through upper half of liver.

Elongated salivary gland under liver.

Anus — wastes ejected into mantle cavity.

Rectum.

Liver produces digestive juice.

Pancreas (not shown) — lies below liver at this position. It is a small diamond-shaped structure that produces digestive enzymes.

Stomach — digestion begins.

Stomach pouch — digestion completed, absorption of digested food into blood takes place here.

Arrows show direction of passage of food and wastes.

Fig. 44. Simplified Digestive System of Squid.

The stomach is a small, thick sac which connects with a large, thin-walled visceral organ, the *stomach pouch,* in which digestion and absorption take place. After a meal the stomach pouch becomes so large that it extends all the way to the tip end of the body. If your specimen was caught when it had not eaten for some time the stomach pouch would be quite small.

Find the spot where the esophagus connects with the stomach (see Fig. 44). Right alongside the stomach pouch is a narrow tube that extends toward the head. This is the intestine. The intestine connects with a small rectum and an opening called the anus. Use the probe to help you find the rectum and anus. Wastes are expelled from the body through the anus.

Above the rectum is the ink sac (see Fig. 43). It opens into the siphon near the anus. When in danger, the squid forces its "ink" into the water and moves away, leaving a dark cloud that conceals it from its enemies.

Respiratory System

Locate the *gills* (see Fig. 43), one on each side of the body. They look like curved feathers pointing toward the head. Water containing dissolved oxygen is taken into the mantle cavity. The water swirls around the gills which are richly supplied with blood vessels. The dissolved oxygen is taken into the blood vessels of the gills. The oxygen-rich blood is then circulated to all parts of the body. Examine the gills with the hand lens to see the blood vessels.

Circulatory System

The squid has three hearts (see Fig. 43). The main one is the *systemic heart* located slightly below the base of the gills. It pumps blood into three main arteries: the *anterior aorta,* which serves the head region; the *posterior aorta,* whose branches serve the mantle, the digestive system and the kidneys, and the *genital artery* which carries blood to the reproductive system. These main vessels have smaller branches that are difficult to trace. The smallest branches are capillaries which are microscopic in size. These run into small veins which finally bring the blood to several main veins, the *anterior* and the *posterior vena cavae* (two of each). The vena cavae deliver blood to the *branchial* (gill) *hearts.* The blood takes on oxygen in the gills and gives up carbon dioxide. From the gills the blood goes back to the systemic heart with new oxygen to start the cycle all over again.

Excretory System

Locate two small triangular bodies at the base of the gills, one on each side of and slightly above the systemic heart (see Fig. 43). These are the kidneys or *nephridia.* Each one has a small opening into the mantle cavity through which liquid wastes are released. Solid wastes are discharged through the anus. (See Fig. 44.)

Head region.

Beak.

Nerve ring around gullet.

Supra buccal ganglion (nerve center at mouth region).

Cerebral ganglion or supra esophageal ganglion.

Gullet or esophagus.

Pen (cartilaginous supporting structure), a modified shell.

Nerves to arms or tentacles.

Infra buccal ganglion (nerve center near mouth).

Propedal ganglion.

Sub-esophageal ganglion.

Visceral ganglion (nerve center controlling digestive system).

Neck region.

Mantle.

Stellate ganglion —center for nerves to mantle and other lower parts of body.

Ganglia in head act as the brain. They connect with stellate ganglia in neck by means of nerves. Nerves from rest of body connect with stellate ganglia centers which serve as relay centers between "brain" and nerve supply of mantle.

Fig. 45. Nervous System (Main Centers) of a Squid.

Nervous System

The main part of the nervous system is in the head and neck where it is most needed. (See Fig. 45.) It is very much like the nervous system of the grasshopper, crayfish and earthworm, consisting of several main ganglia (nerve centers) connectives and nerves that go to all parts of the body. In live squid the large *stellate* (star shaped) *ganglia* are visible through the transparent lining of the mantle where the neck and mantle meet.

Recent investigations have shown that the squid has giant sized nerve fibers that make excellent subjects for the study of nerve reactions.

Step 1. With forceps lift mantle above siphon and cut with scissors as shown.

Step 2. Cut along middle of mantle until you reach an obstruction. This obstruction is the pen which is the transformed shell, part of the inner skeleton.

ANTERIOR

Mantle.

Siphon.

Pen or inner skeleton.

POSTERIOR.

Step 3. Cut around and on both sides of this "obstruction" and separate the mantle.

Step 4. Remove the pen by lifting it with forceps and pulling towards head.

Fig. 46. Removing the Pen—A Part of the Squid's Inner Skeleton.

Skeletal System

The squid is an invertebrate with an endoskeleton or inner skeleton. This is most unusual because normally only vertebrates have an endoskeleton. After you have completed the dissection and identified the internal organs, remove the pins that hold the mantle to the dissecting pan. Roll the cut mantle back to its original shape and position. Pin the two loose edges together. Turn the squid over completely so that its anterior (see Fig. 40) surface faces up, and remove the inner shell or *pen* as shown on Fig. 46. You will remember the squid is related to the clam. The pen of the squid is really a shell that has been modified and encased in tissue.

The squid has a casing of cartilage tissue in the head that is somewhat like the cartilage that covers the brain of the shark, which is a vertebrate animal. The squid also has internal cartilage supports in the mantle tissue.

Reproductive System

Squid are either male or female. With Fig. 43 as a guide let's study the reproductive system.

The male organs: Near the rectum is a tube through which sperm cells are discharged. This tube connects with a complicated tube called the *vas deferens* that extends down below the gills and there connects with the testis, a large, long gland that produces the sperm cells.

The female organs: Alongside the left branchial heart is a swollen sac called the *oviducal gland.* This connects with a long, coiled tube called the *oviduct* which is filled with eggs during the breeding season. If you have a female squid, try cutting the oviduct with a razor and examining the eggs with a low power microscope (50x to 100x) or with a 5x hand lens. Note the large mass that looks like a cluster of many tiny pearls. The oviduct runs into a large, lobed gland, the *ovary,* which is located above the stomach pouch and extends to the tip of the body.

In our discussion of the squid we learned that the snail and the squid, two very unlike forms (see Fig. 40, page 70), belong to the same major group of animals, the *Mollusca.* The following projects will help you expand your knowledge about these animals.

Project 1: Cockles, Mussels and Devilfish

Try dissecting the clam and the octopus to help round out the picture of this strange and important group of animals. Follow the same general directions in dissecting the octopus as you did for the squid. Obtain an injected specimen of *Octopus vulgaris.*

For the clam dissection get an injected *Anadontia mutabilis,* a fresh water clam or mussel. Bear in mind that the foot, a fleshy extension between the shells or valves, is comparable to the head and neck of the squid, and that the pen of the squid is actually a reduction or modification of the shell of the clam. The general body plan is comparable in both types.

Project 2: A Living Wood Drill—The Shipworm

The shipworm or *teredo* is not a worm. It is a member of the molluscs with a modified toothed shell. The shell is located at the front of the body and is used by the animal for boring chambers into wood. It destroys wooden hulls of ships, piles, docks and wharves, particularly in the tropical and subtropical zones.

Obtain a specimen of wood containing live shipworms or *Teredo navalis*. Remove one from its wood chamber and dissect it, using the same general procedure as you used in dissecting the squid. You will see remarkable adaptations for its strange way of life. The February 1961 issue of *Scientific American* has an article on the shipworm which provides excellent illustrations that may be used as a guide for this dissection.

Project 3:   Studying Heartbeat of Mussel and Snail

Obtain a live clam. Crack open but do not smash one of the shells. A small hammer will do. Using a scalpel, cut through the muscles that hold the shell to the body. Remove the white sheet of mantle tissue from the internal organs. The heart will be seen pulsating. Bathe the exposed area with sea water or artificial sea water to keep it from drying out. See page 65, Project 1, for information on artificial sea water.

You can test the effects of common household drugs like aspirin, bufferin, etc. on the heartbeat of the clam. Just grind and dissolve a pill in about ½ glass of water. Place a drop of the solution over the heart and await results. Try experimenting with chemicals such as urethane, glutathione, cortisone, magnesium sulfate, adrenalin, insulin, etc.

The snail, *Lymnaea stagnalis* can also be used for observing heart action. Only young snails will show the heartbeat satisfactorily. (The number of bands on the shell of a snail reveals its age; the fewer bands on the shell, the younger the snail.) Try boring a hole in the top of the snail's shell and flashing a pen light into the opening, to get better observations.

This chapter has taken us from the monster squid, the rocket of the sea, which roams the seas as the hunter and the hunted, to the shipworm, a minute animal that lives in its self-created tomb.

The squid family has become important because of the many research investigations being carried on with them. At Woods Hole in Cape Cod, exciting things are being done with molluscs under the auspices of The Marine Biological Institute for Research and by the Oceanographic Institute.

We have examined the major patterns of invertebrate life from the earthworm to the squid. Let us now look at an important primitive vertebrate, the shark.

7

A Boneless Fish —
The Sandshark or Dogfish Shark.

THROUGHOUT the world of the sea there roams a powerful creature, the shark, whose very name excites fear and horror. Yet there are few types of sharks that will attack a human without provocation. The dogfish shark, like other sharks, is a scavenger, feeding chiefly on dead matter. Most sharks are relatively harmless to man but all sharks are a source of irritation to the commercial fisherman because they prey upon the fish he wants to catch and so interfere with his livelihood.

A study of the history of living things from prehistoric time shows that sharks have always successfully inhabited the seas. Fossil evidences reveal that the shark was prominent hundreds of millions of years ago as he is today. While other primitive forms were much modified and became extinct with the climatic changes that have altered the earth's interior and surface structure, the shark lives on as one of the most evolutionally successful forms of life ever produced. Why is this so?

The shark has been so successful because it is relatively free to roam the seas, for which he is excellently suited by his streamlined form and great strength. Another reason is that sharks protect their young by carrying them in their bodies until the young sharks are almost fully formed. This protection helps the group to survive since few of the young are destroyed by other animals. The shark's body is a highly muscular machine and its scales form a tough armor. In fact the scales are really primitive teeth, and the fearsome teeth in the mouth of the shark are actually modified scales (see Fig. 47).

Most fish have bones that form an inner skeleton, as many of us have unhappily discovered at the dinner table. However, the sharks and the rays (primitive fish closely related to sharks) do not have bony skeletons. Instead their inner skeleton or *endoskeleton* is composed of a tissue called *cartilage*. While cartilage is softer than bone it still has the quality of toughness. It has yet another important property, it is somewhat flexible. This permits great freedom of bodily motion. To get some idea of the properties of cartilage, hold the upper part of your ear between two fingers and then twist it. The same kind of tissue that is under the skin of your ear makes up the endoskeleton of both the small dogfish shark and of the giant basking shark which reaches a length of forty feet! The shark, like the ray, is a primitive fish. The cartilaginous skeleton in the shark is a forerunner of the bony skeleton found in higher types of fish like the herring.

Menu for a Shark

One of the unceasing challenges facing all animals is the fateful problem of survival—to get food or to become food. Many animals have difficulty in surviving because their diet is very limited. For example, deer are vegetarians; if a prolonged and heavy snowfall blankets their food they starve. But sharks are omnivorous; that is, they will eat almost anything. In fact studies of the contents of sharks' stomachs have shown some remarkable things such as tin cans, indigestible rubbish thrown overboard from boats and many other unlikely foods. The shark can get rid of such indigestible matter because it has an *evertible digestive organ;* that is, a part of its intestine that can turn itself inside out. (See Fig. 51 and page 86: the *spiral valve*.) That is how the shark discharges indigestible objects like fish bones and other wastes from its body.

Segments and Gills

Do you remember the segments of the earthworm described on page 17? All vertebrates, even man, are built on the segment plan. Segments are hard to see in man because they become modified as he grows from an early embryo stage to a late embryo stage. All these changes take place before the human baby is born. Segments may be observed in the segmented gill arches of a human embryo which are comparable to those of a fish.

Segments are strikingly shown in all vertebrate embryos

Rows of sharp tipped scales (enlarged) — tips point backward. Scales are embedded in skin and continue into mouth where they are specialized as teeth. The teeth, like the scales, are superficial and have no roots.

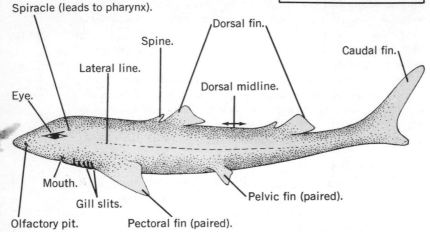

Spiracle (leads to pharynx).

Dorsal fin.

Spine.

Lateral line.

Dorsal midline.

Caudal fin.

Eye.

Mouth.

Gill slits.

Olfactory pit.

Pectoral fin (paired).

Pelvic fin (paired).

Fig. 47. External Anatomy (Side View) of Dogfish Shark.

by the arrangement of masses of muscle in sections, each of which is called a *myotome*. You can see myotomes when you open a can of salmon. They are the pink sections that you eat. The segmental arrangement of muscles in the salmon is very much like that in the dogfish shark. Segments in the dogfish shark show clearly in the gill slits and gill arches. (See Figs. 47 and 55.)

Since the dogfish shark lives only in water we are not surprised to find that it has no lungs and breathes by means of gills. You may ask why a whale, which also lives in water, has lungs and no gills. The answer is that the whale is a mammal, not a fish. Its ancestors were "landlubbers" with four legs. Like all mammal embryos including man, the embryo whale has gill slits.

Unlike most fish the dogfish shark is a livebearer; that is, it develops its young inside the body instead of discharging its eggs to develop into fish outside the body. The young dogfish shark is often called a *puppy*. You will find out more about the puppy when you do your dissection. It is important

82

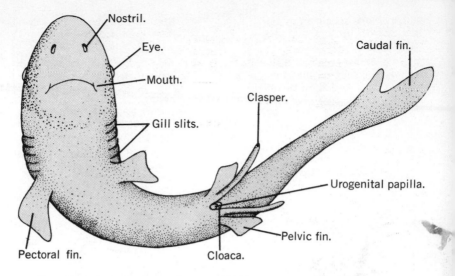

Fig. 48. External Anatomy (Ventral View) of Male Dogfish Shark.

to study the shark because a dissection of the shark reveals the vertebrate pattern of structure in its basic primitive form.

Dissecting the Dogfish Shark

Obtain two specimens of the dogfish shark *Squalus acanthias,* one male and one female, from 12 to 18 inches long. If the female is carrying a developing baby shark you can actually study three specimens, the male, the female and the puppy. The male dogfish shark has *claspers* which he uses to channel or direct the sperm (male sex cells) into the female's reproductive chamber; the female dogfish shark does not have claspers.

In order to perform the dissection you will need the same equipment you used for the earthworm dissection, a pair of sharp curved surgical scissors about 6 inches long, a smooth metal probe about 6 inches long and a large dissecting pan or board about 20 inches long. You will also need a roll of plastic wrap or aluminum foil to wrap the specimens when you are not working with them so that they do not dry out. A magnifying lens one inch or more in diameter is important to help locate and trace nerves and blood vessels, and a pen flashlight helps to trace the origin of small vessels and to locate small apertures. We are now ready to examine and dissect the dogfish shark.

83

Step 1. Place specimen in pan ventral side up and pin pectoral fins as shown.

Step 2. Using scalpel make midline incision cutting from point A to E and E to B. Cut through body wall but not through underlying membrane.

Step 3. Cut from point A to C on each side and from E to D on each side.

Step 4. Roll back flaps of body wall. Use probe or scalpel to free body wall from any adhering tissue. Pin to pan as shown at point X and Y. Use fine scissors to cut away membrane.

Step 5. Refer to Fig. 50 to see main cavities in which organs are found.

Fig. 49. Opening Abdominal Cavity of Dogfish Shark.

External Anatomy of the Dogfish Shark

Place the male dogfish shark on the dissecting pan, dorsal side up. (Mouth is on the ventral side.) Locate on the specimen the unpaired fins or single fins on the dorsal midline, the paired pectoral fins, and the single tail or caudal fin (see Fig. 47). Locate all labeled apertures or openings on the dorsal and ventral surfaces of the head and on the ventral side between the pelvic fins (see Fig. 48). Examples of apertures are spiracles, mouth, gill slits, nostrils and cloaca.

Turn the dogfish ventral side up (mouth upward) to examine the under part of the specimen. Identify on the specimen the following parts labeled in Fig. 48: pair of pectoral fins, pair of pelvic fins, pair of claspers and caudal fin. Uneven lobes in the caudal fin are characteristic of all sharks.

Opening the Abdominal Cavity

The specimen that you receive has a deep transverse or

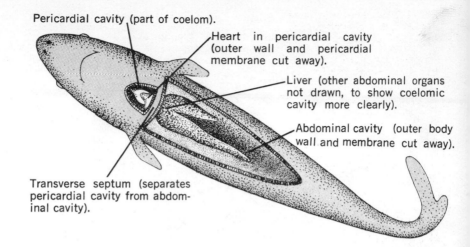

Pericardial cavity (part of coelom).

Heart in pericardial cavity (outer wall and pericardial membrane cut away).

Liver (other abdominal organs not drawn, to show coelomic cavity more clearly).

Abdominal cavity (outer body wall and membrane cut away).

Transverse septum (separates pericardial cavity from abdominal cavity).

Fig. 50. Body Cavities in the Dogfish Shark.

crosswise cut in the tail region. Cut the tail piece off at this point with a scalpel. Then dissect and peel back about 2 inches of the skin on the cut off tail piece. Use probe to help separate the skin from the muscles. You will see the segmental arrangement of muscles or myotomes. Save the tail piece for study of a vertebra or spinal bone (see Project 3, page 96). Now follow directions for opening the abdominal cavity as given in Fig. 49.

Body Cavities in the Dogfish Shark

All animals from the earthworm to man have an internal cavity called the *coelom*. Consult Fig. 50 to see the two main body cavities in which the major organs are found.

Digestive System of the Dogfish Shark

To understand how the shark's digestive system functions we will follow the digestive organs in the specimen, with the aid of the diagram in Fig. 51 which shows the abdominal organs.

Food entering the *mouth* passes through the *pharynx* and through the *esophagus*. The pharynx and esophagus are not shown in Fig. 51 because they are not found in the abdominal cavity. Food enters the *stomach* from the esophagus. Digestion begins in the stomach. Partially digested food leaves the stomach, passes through the *duodenum* where digestive en-

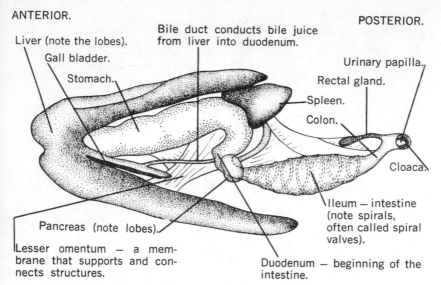

ANTERIOR.   POSTERIOR.

Liver (note the lobes).   Bile duct conducts bile juice
                             from liver into duodenum.

Gall bladder.   Urinary papilla.

Stomach.   Rectal gland.

                                                             Spleen.

                                                             Colon.

                                                                        Cloaca.

                                                             Ileum — intestine
                                                             (note spirals,
Pancreas (note lobes).   often called spiral
                                                             valves).

Lesser omentum — a mem-
brane that supports and con-   Duodenum — beginning of the
nects structures.   intestine.

Fig. 51. Digestive System (Abdominal Organs) of the Dogfish Shark.

zymes from the *pancreas* continue the digestion of food, and enters the *ileum* (intestine) where digestion is completed.

The *liver*, made up of 3 main divisions or lobes, secretes bile juice which empties into the duodenum through the bile duct. Bile juice helps in the digestion of fatty foods.

The pancreas has an upper lobe and a lower lobe. It sends a digestive secretion into the duodenum.

After the food is digested, solid wastes pass out of the ileum through the *colon* into the *cloaca* which is a chamber that opens to the outside of the body. The cloaca also receives liquid wastes from the *urinary ducts* which terminate in the *urinary papilla,* and sex cells from the reproductive organs. (See Figs. 56 and 57.) Solid and liquid wastes are expelled from the cloaca through the cloacal opening.

The *spiral valve* is a muscular sac inside the ileum or intestine which turns itself inside out through the cloacal opening like the waste bag in a vacuum cleaner and empties its store of indigestible wastes into the ocean.

The *spleen,* although one of the abdominal organs, is not considered a part of the digestive system. It is actually a part of the lymphatic system, a division of the circulatory system. Little is known about the physiology of the spleen.

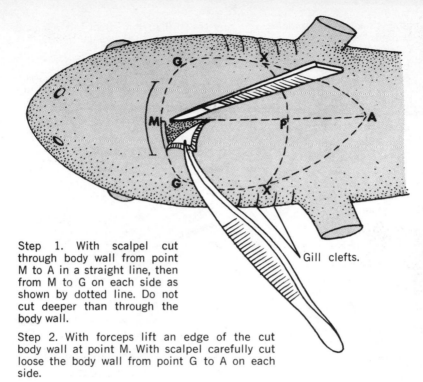

Step 1. With scalpel cut through body wall from point M to A in a straight line, then from M to G on each side as shown by dotted line. Do not cut deeper than through the body wall.

Gill clefts.

Step 2. With forceps lift an edge of the cut body wall at point M. With scalpel carefully cut loose the body wall from point G to A on each side.

Step 3. With scissors cut off the loosened body wall. Follow the dotted curve MGA on each side of body as you cut.

Step 4. The pericardial sac containing the heart is now exposed. With scalpel cut open this thin-walled sac from point A to P and from P to X on each side.

Step 5. Carefully dissect away muscles in area from M to P, above dotted lines XPX, up to gill clefts on both sides. Avoid cutting large blood vessels and nerves.

Fig. 52. How to Expose the Heart and Main Veins.

How to Expose the Heart and Main Veins

To learn how the shark's heart is constructed we are going to expose the heart and the important veins of the circulatory system. This will require the scalpel, forceps, probe and a pair of straight scissors. Follow the steps indicated in Fig. 52. What the circulatory system looks like after the dissection is

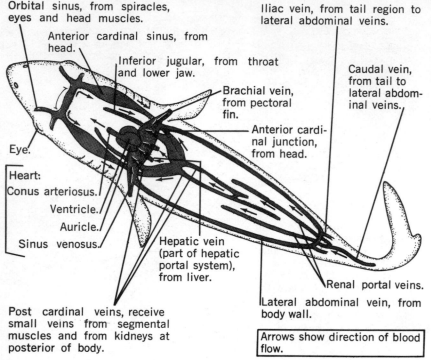

Orbital sinus, from spiracles, eyes and head muscles.

Anterior cardinal sinus, from head.

Inferior jugular, from throat and lower jaw.

Brachial vein, from pectoral fin.

Iliac vein, from tail region to lateral abdominal veins.

Caudal vein, from tail to lateral abdominal veins.

Anterior cardinal junction, from head.

Eye.

Heart:
Conus arteriosus.
Ventricle.
Auricle.
Sinus venosus.

Hepatic vein (part of hepatic portal system), from liver.

Post cardinal veins, receive small veins from segmental muscles and from kidneys at posterior of body.

Renal portal veins.

Lateral abdominal vein, from body wall.

Arrows show direction of blood flow.

Fig. 53. Main Veins of Dogfish Shark—Simplified Diagram.

completed is shown by Fig. 53. After the digestive system is exposed, move it aside to locate all the main veins. Note that the veins in the specimen appear blue. They were injected by the supplier with a blue dye to help us trace the circulatory system. Use Fig. 53 as a guide in studying the veins.

Find the *sinus venosus,* an antechamber of the heart. Trace the veins that lead to the sinus venosus. Begin at the sinus venosus and follow the veins back to the body parts where they originate. Slit open the sinus venosus with a sharp scalpel or a razor blade, from left to right along its ventral side, to see where the veins enter the heart. Lift each vein with a fine probe to help you trace its course.

Hepatic Portal System of the Dogfish Shark

How does the digested food reach all parts of the body of the dogfish shark? This is accomplished as follows: the digested food is transported from the digestive organs (stom-

88

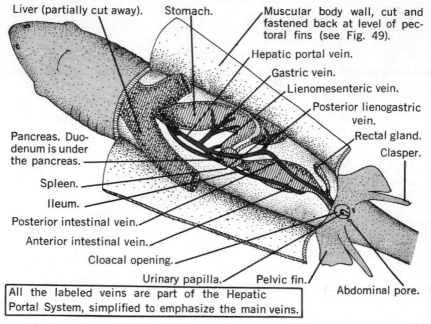

Liver (partially cut away).   Stomach.   Muscular body wall, cut and fastened back at level of pectoral fins (see Fig. 49).

Hepatic portal vein.

Gastric vein.

Lienomesenteric vein.

Posterior lienogastric vein.

Rectal gland.

Clasper.

Pancreas. Duodenum is under the pancreas.

Spleen.

Ileum.

Posterior intestinal vein.

Anterior intestinal vein.

Cloacal opening.

Urinary papilla.   Pelvic fin.

Abdominal pore.

All the labeled veins are part of the Hepatic Portal System, simplified to emphasize the main veins.

Fig. 54. Simplified Hepatic Portal System of Dogfish Shark.

ach, duodenum and ileum) through veins of the *hepatic portal system*. (Hepatic means pertaining to the liver.) From the liver the blood containing the digested food flows through hepatic veins into the sinus venosus. The blood then goes from the sinus venosus into the heart which pumps the blood through the arteries to all parts of the body.

Fig. 54 shows a simplified version of the hepatic portal system emphasizing the main veins. With the aid of the diagram locate the veins of the hepatic portal system in your specimen.

The Main Arteries of the Dogfish Shark

We have examined the system of veins in the dogfish shark. Now let us examine the system of arteries which serve only one purpose, to deliver blood to the organs. To study the arteries of the dogfish shark we are going to continue the dissection, following the procedure described below:

Trace the arteries in the abdominal section from the heart to the main organs they service. Make an incision with the

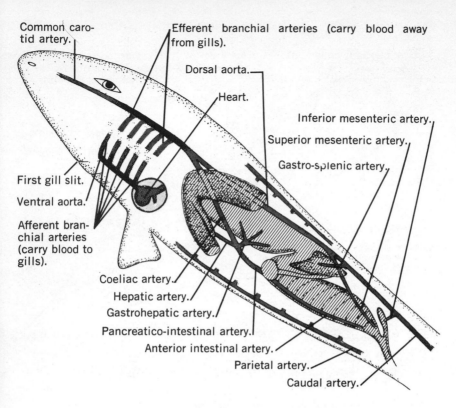

Fig. 55. Main Arteries of the Dogfish Shark.

scalpel from one corner of the mouth to the first gill slit on one side of the head. Lift the skin with forceps and separate it from the underlying tissue with a scalpel and probe until the skin is free from the mouth up to the first gill slit. Lift the exposed sections of muscles until the blood vessels around the gills are exposed. Be careful not to cut any large nerves or blood vessels. The nerves are white in color. In your specimen the arteries contain a red dye while the veins contain a blue dye. Follow the arteries with a probe. Use scalpel and probe to free the arteries from any adhering tissue in the anterior end (the head). Using Fig. 55 as a guide, determine which organ is served by each of the main arteries labeled in the illustration.

Reproductive Organs of the Male Dogfish Shark

Fig. 56 illustrates the reproductive organs of the male

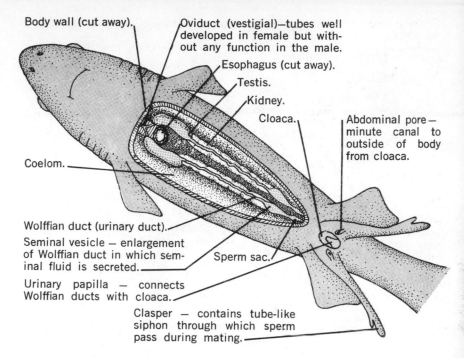

Body wall (cut away).

Oviduct (vestigial)—tubes well developed in female but without any function in the male.

Esophagus (cut away).

Testis.

Kidney.

Cloaca.

Abdominal pore — minute canal to outside of body from cloaca.

Coelom.

Wolffian duct (urinary duct).

Seminal vesicle — enlargement of Wolffian duct in which seminal fluid is secreted.

Sperm sac.

Urinary papilla — connects Wolffian ducts with cloaca.

Clasper — contains tube-like siphon through which sperm pass during mating.

Fig. 56. Urogenital System (Excretory and Reproductive) of Male Dogfish Shark.

dogfish. To locate these organs in the specimen lift the liver and move its lobes aside. Do the same thing with the digestive organs. The *urogenital system* (excretory and reproductive organs) will then be seen.

The testes produce sex cells called sperm. The sperm cell has a tail or *flagellum* that enables it to swim from the testes through small tubes into the *Wolffian duct*. In the male dogfish shark the Wolffian duct, in addition to sperm cells, carries urine from the kidneys to the cloaca. In the female the Wolffian duct transports only urine.

From the Wolffian duct of the male the sperm cells enter the *seminal vesicles* and *sperm sacs* for temporary storage. During mating the sperm cells are discharged from the sperm sacs through the cloaca, through the *urinary papilla* and along a channel on the claspers to the cloaca of the female dogfish.

Reproductive Organs of the Female Dogfish Shark

After the sperm cells of the male dogfish shark unite with

91

REPRODUCTIVE PARTS:

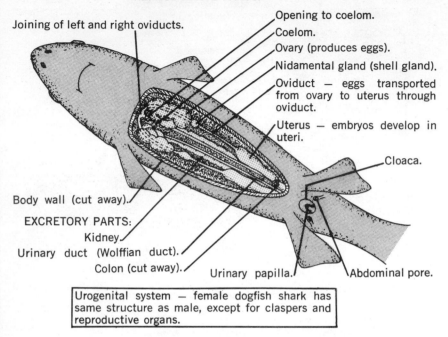

Joining of left and right oviducts.

Opening to coelom.

Coelom.

Ovary (produces eggs).

Nidamental gland (shell gland).

Oviduct — eggs transported from ovary to uterus through oviduct.

Uterus — embryos develop in uteri.

Cloaca.

Body wall (cut away).

EXCRETORY PARTS:

Kidney.

Urinary duct (Wolffian duct).

Colon (cut away).

Urinary papilla.

Abdominal pore.

Urogenital system — female dogfish shark has same structure as male, except for claspers and reproductive organs.

Fig. 57. Urogenital System (Excretory and Reproductive) of Female Dogfish Shark.

eggs of the female the fertilized eggs develop within the *uteri* (singular, uterus) of the female's body into young sharks or puppies. The puppies develop a food sac or *yolk sac* on their ventral, abdominal section which provides food for the young shark until he is discharged from the mother's body to go hunting for his own food.

What are the female shark's reproductive organs? The reproductive system of the female dogfish shark is the basic pattern for the reproductive systems of all higher vertebrate animal forms.

To dissect the female dogfish shark follow the same directions given in Figs. 49 and 52 for the dissection of the male dogfish shark. Move the liver and the digestive organs aside to expose the reproductive organs. Note the absence of claspers in the female dogfish shark. Starting at the ovaries, identify parts of the reproductive system of the female dogfish as labeled in Fig. 57.

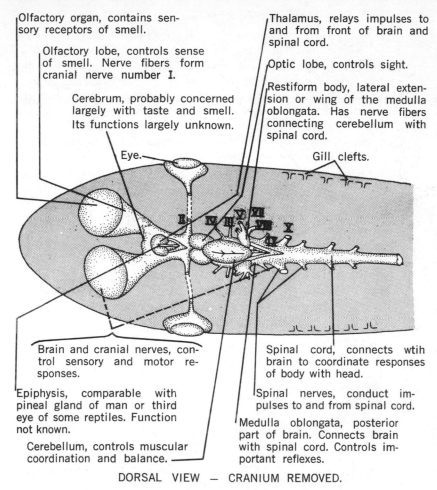

Olfactory organ, contains sensory receptors of smell.

Olfactory lobe, controls sense of smell. Nerve fibers form cranial nerve number I.

Cerebrum, probably concerned largely with taste and smell. Its functions largely unknown.

Eye.

Thalamus, relays impulses to and from front of brain and spinal cord.

Optic lobe, controls sight.

Restiform body, lateral extension or wing of the medulla oblongata. Has nerve fibers connecting cerebellum with spinal cord.

Gill clefts.

Brain and cranial nerves, control sensory and motor responses.

Epiphysis, comparable with pineal gland of man or third eye of some reptiles. Function not known.

Cerebellum, controls muscular coordination and balance.

Spinal cord, connects wtih brain to coordinate responses of body with head.

Spinal nerves, conduct impulses to and from spinal cord.

Medulla oblongata, posterior part of brain. Connects brain with spinal cord. Controls important reflexes.

DORSAL VIEW — CRANIUM REMOVED.

Fig. 58. Main Parts of Nervous System of Dogfish Shark.

Dissection of the female shark is especially interesting if the specimen contains developing young. Cut open each uterus and examine the contents for possible developing embryos or puppies.

Nervous System of the Dogfish Shark

Can the shark think? Does he have a high I. Q.? When we examine the nervous system of the dogfish shark (see Fig. 58) we find that he definitely has a brain which is far more

93

advanced than that of the invertebrates we have studied. However, it is primitive and poorly developed compared to the brain in the higher vertebrates. The shark's brain is very much like the human brain in elementary pattern but the main parts are not developed to the same degree as in the human brain. For instance, the cerebrum or thinking and association area is greatly developed in man but in the dogfish shark it is small and poorly developed. On the other hand the olfactory area that controls the sense of smell is very large in the shark's brain but is quite small in the human brain. The dogfish shark has 10 pairs of cranial nerves (see Fig. 58) that control the sensory and motor activities of the head and some other parts of the body. Man has 12 pairs of cranial nerves that perform similar functions. These examples are enough to show some of the principal changes that took place in the evolution of the nervous system as more advanced vertebrate animals appeared on the earth.

We are going to expose the nervous system of the dogfish shark by following the procedure described below:

Place the dogfish shark on pan dorsal side up. Cut away all the skin from top of head to last gill clefts. Remove the cranium (cartilaginous covering over brain) by slicing away very thin flat sections of cartilage with a sharp scalpel until the brain is exposed. Be very careful not to cut any nerves, especially near the eyes. The nerves look like thin white cords. Some nerves pass through the cartilage.

Locate the main parts of the brain (see Fig. 58) and the connection of each part with the spinal cord. The *medulla oblongata* is the end of the brain and connects with the spinal cord. The spinal cord has paired spinal nerves.

After dissecting the shark it would be valuable to dissect the perch, a bony fish, to highlight the evolutionary change in endoskeleton from cartilage to bone.

Some Interesting Projects

Did you ever stop to think that there is a connection between the kind of environment animals live in and the type of organs they have? Here is a suggestion for making a comparative study of hearts of various animals to test this relationship.

Project 1: A Comparative Study of Hearts

Make a collection of vertebrate hearts. Begin with the lowest vertebrates like the dogfish shark or other fish. To remove the heart follow the same general procedures given in Fig. 52. Photograph each heart and then preserve it by putting it into a jar filled with a 10% formalin solution. Dissect out the heart of preserved amphibia specimens such as the frog and the necturus, and of various reptiles such as turtles and snakes. (See Chapter 8: The Fabulous Frog, page 108.) Remove the heart from a chicken or other fowl that is planned for the gala Sunday dinner. Try to get a cow's heart from a butcher shop or slaughter house.

Dissect each heart to show the main parts. Show how the hearts of warm-blooded animals like the bird, represented by the chicken heart, and the cow, differ from the hearts of cold-blooded animals such as the dogfish shark and the frog. How does the heart structure of amphibia, which live part of their lives in water and part on land, differ from the hearts of landliving vertebrates?

Project 2: Tips from Scales

Each major group of fish has its own kind of scales. The scale of the dogfish shark is called a *placoid* scale. The perch has *ctenoid* scales. Other animals like the reptiles, birds and mammals also have some kind of scales. Birds' feathers are related to scales and birds have scales on their legs. Even man has tiny scales on his hairs.

You can make a fascinating project of preserving and photographing scales. After a while you can determine the group to which an animal belongs with only a scale as evidence.

Fish scales may be softened for study under a microscope by soaking them in glycerine overnight. They may then be examined with a microscope using 100x magnification. Scales may be photographed and later preserved in formaldehyde. No soaking in g'ˈcerine is necessary to preserve the scales.

Scales on human hair should be studied under a high power microscope (400x to 1000x magnification). Place a single hair on a slide and add a drop of water to hold the hair in place. Microphotographs of human hair may be taken to show the scales which are arranged around the outermost part of the shaft of the hair. Compare the scales of human hair with scales on hair taken from other mammals such as rabbits, dogs, cats, etc. A variety of mammal hairs can also be obtained from old pieces of fur.

Project 3: How to Tell a Tale from Head to Tail

Obtain vertebrae (individual sections of the spinal column) from members of the main groups of vertebrates: fish, amphibia, reptiles, birds and mammals. You can save vertebrae from your dissections and get others from biological supply houses. A visit to a museum will give you a chance to photograph vertebrae of prehistoric animals like dinosaurs. Arrange the vertebrae and the photographs to show group relationships from the simplest group of vertebrates like the fish to the most complex groups like birds and mammals. Visit the library to get books on comparative anatomy and learn the differences in vertebrae structure. Now select any vertebra and build a true tale around it. To what group does it belong? How large was the animal to whom the vertebra belonged? Was it a quadruped, a bird or a bat? How good a science detective are you?

Project 4: Investigating Evolution In The Aquarium

Not all research is done in a laboratory. Libraries, aquaria, museums, and field studies provide fascinating settings for discovery. In this experiment, you can use several of these sources to investigate the principle of evolutionary adaptation among fish.

In all of the great animal groups (the phyla), we find that the organisms evolved in order to adapt to diverse conditions in their environment. Among mammals we see animals that fly, swim, burrow, run, climb, etc. Similarly, among birds there are divers, swimmers, high fliers, and wingless walkers. In all cases the limbs, as well as other parts, have become adapted to the organism's novel means of locomotion.

Here is an interesting aquarium project: study the adaptations of fins among fish. There, and in museums, you will find fish alive or preserved that have explored all the possibilities of life in or close to a water environment. Bring your camera or sketching pad and record fish that live in mud (lungfish), bottom crawlers, flying fish, strong pelagic swimmers, etc. Draw or photograph and study the fin structures; then compare them with the limbs of birds and mammals.

The Fabulous Frog. 8

MAN OWES a great debt to the frog. For generations the frog has contributed to our knowledge of anatomy, physiology, embryology, parasitology and many other of the important "ologies." This lowly vertebrate, almost comical in appearance, has been an old standby among scientists, in the school classroom and in the professional laboratory, and will continue to be a well for drawing knowledge in the science of life. It is an animal that survives well in captivity and is easily handled.

The frog leads a double life. As a tadpole, before maturity, it is an aquanaut, a water dweller breathing by gills; as an adult it is a terranaut, a lung-breathing land dweller. However, because its eggs are laid in water and because there are no protective scales on its skin, the adult frog must live in moist surroundings near a source of water. Skin divers have learned from the frog, with its webbed toes, how to propel themselves rapidly in water. In fact skin divers are sometimes called frogmen.

The class of vertebrates, *Amphibia*, of which the frog is a member, includes salamanders, toads and worm-like creatures called caecilians. They are an ancient and venerable group; one might say they are almost living fossils. Once a great and dominant group, they are now the smallest group of vertebrates. Their legacy to the progress of evolution was to serve as ancestor of the reptiles which, in turn, gave rise to birds and mammals and finally to man, a representative of the mammals. Now their evolutionary job appears to be done. Even today there is evidence of their ancient greatness. Japan has a salamander that grows to five feet in length and weighs up to 100 pounds. At the other end of the scale is a Cuban frog, all of ⅜ of an inch long.

Fig. 59. American Bullfrog (Rana Catesbiana).
Courtesy American Museum of Natural History.

Certain of the amphibia are of great economic value to man. For instance, the giant South American toad can eat, in one month, up to 3000 or more insects harmful to man. For this reason the South American giant toad has been exported to the Hawaiian Islands to combat the grubs that destroy sugar cane. Another example of the frogs' value to man is evidenced by the practice of stocking lakes with tadpoles, in mosquito control programs, because they eat mosquito larvae or wrigglers.

In many respects the anatomy of the frog is similar to the anatomy of man. A study of the frog's anatomy gives us a good idea of the main features of human anatomy. It also reveals basic evolutionary differences between the structure of a cold-blooded, fairly primitive vertebrate and the structure of an advanced warm-blooded vertebrate like man. It also highlights the difference between a true amphibian with a three-chambered heart and a true lung-breathing terranaut, like man, with his four-chambered heart.

Let's Prepare for the Dissection

Obtain a double-injected male and egg-bearing female American Bullfrog, *Rana catesbiana,* the largest American frog, or the leopard frog, *Rana pipiens,* smaller and less costly. Do not get the pickerel frog (which looks like the leopard frog) because its skin produces a secretion that causes allergic re-actions in some people, resulting in inflammation of the skin on the hands.

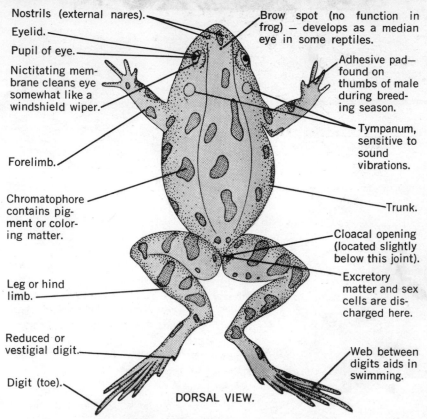

Nostrils (external nares).

Eyelid.

Pupil of eye.

Nictitating membrane cleans eye somewhat like a windshield wiper.

Forelimb.

Chromatophore contains pigment or coloring matter.

Leg or hind limb.

Reduced or vestigial digit.

Digit (toe).

Brow spot (no function in frog) — develops as a median eye in some reptiles.

Adhesive pad—found on thumbs of male during breeding season.

Tympanum, sensitive to sound vibrations.

Trunk.

Cloacal opening (located slightly below this joint).

Excretory matter and sex cells are discharged here.

Web between digits aids in swimming.

DORSAL VIEW.

Fig. 60. External Anatomy of Male Frog.

You will require the basic dissection equipment used for the earthworm, plus a pen flashlight or pen flashlight magnifier, a wooden matchstick, a pair of strong 3½ inch scissors with one blunt tip and one sharp tip, and a bristle from a nylon hairbrush.

Exploring the External Anatomy of the Frog

Place the frog dorsal side up in the dissecting pan. Stroke the skin with your finger and feel its smoothness. Examine the skin with your hand lens to note the absence of scales. The frog breathes through its moist skin, diffusing oxygen into the tiny blood vessels in the skin. It also breathes by means of lungs (see Fig. 73).

To familiarize yourself with the frog use Fig. 60 as a guide

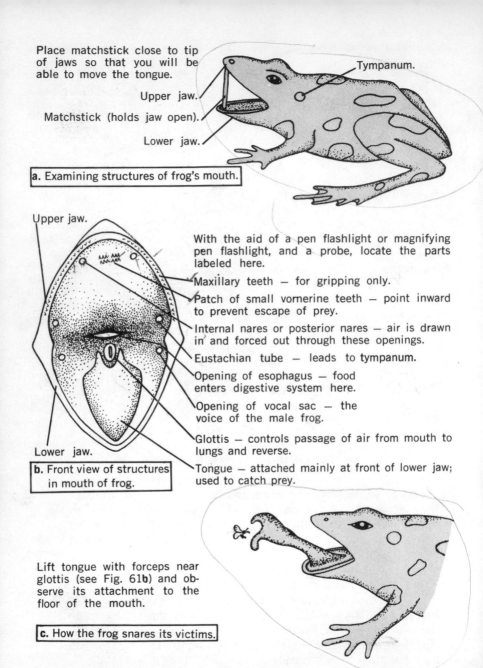

Place matchstick close to tip of jaws so that you will be able to move the tongue.

Tympanum.

Upper jaw.

Matchstick (holds jaw open).

Lower jaw.

a. Examining structures of frog's mouth.

Upper jaw.

With the aid of a pen flashlight or magnifying pen flashlight, and a probe, locate the parts labeled here.

Maxillary teeth — for gripping only.

Patch of small vomerine teeth — point inward to prevent escape of prey.

Internal nares or posterior nares — air is drawn in and forced out through these openings.

Eustachian tube — leads to tympanum.

Opening of esophagus — food enters digestive system here.

Opening of vocal sac — the voice of the male frog.

Glottis — controls passage of air from mouth to lungs and reverse.

Lower jaw.

b. Front view of structures in mouth of frog.

Tongue — attached mainly at front of lower jaw; used to catch prey.

Lift tongue with forceps near glottis (see Fig. 61**b**) and observe its attachment to the floor of the mouth.

c. How the frog snares its victims.

Fig. 61. The Mouth of the Frog.

100

and identify the labeled parts of the diagram on your specimen. Then turn the specimen ventral side up and notice the difference in coloration on its ventral side. These color differences and color patterns help the frog to blend into the background of his natural habitat on land and in water. This protective camouflage has prevented many a frog from becoming a tasty tidbit for a snake.

Let's look into that awesome cavern, the frog's mouth. Fig. 61 (a and b) shows how to prepare the specimen for the study of the structures in the mouth cavity. Insert a fine, firm strand from a nylon hairbrush into one of the Eustachian tubes and watch the *tympanum* or eardrum on the dorsal side of the frog. You will see the tip of the strand pressing upward against the tympanum. This primitive hearing system allows air pressure to be equalized in the head of the frog. It acts as an aerostat. Your male specimen will have two vocal sac openings, one on each side (see Fig. 61b). Place a narrow-tipped medicine dropper at the opening and vigorously force air into the sac. If you then press gently with your fingers under the lower jaw, you may hear the voice in a somewhat ghostly way. Later, after the dissection of all systems except the nervous system has been completed, force air into the *glottis* as you did into the vocal sac. If this frog were not preserved, you'd be surprised to see how large the lungs can then become. Preservation causes tissues which are normally elastic to lose their elasticity.

It is interesting to know how the frog snares its victims. Fig. 61c shows how the tongue is attached, and Fig. 62 shows how the frog captures his food.

Fig. 62. Frog Snaring Insect With Tongue.
Photo by M. F. Roberts from "Natural History".

Step 1. Pin frog to dissecting pan ventral side up as shown.

Step 2. Lift skin with forceps at point C and make shallow cut through lifted skin with a razor or scalpel.

Step 3. Insert rounded edge of scissors into incision and cut skin along dotted line to point X.

Step 4. Make lateral cuts from point A to B and B^1. Then cut down from point C to D and D^1.

Fig. 63. First Steps in Opening Body Cavity of the Frog.

The Inside Story of the Frog's Anatomy

Remove the matchstick from the frog's mouth. Place the frog on the dissecting pan ventral side up. Now follow the directions in Fig. 63. After this is finished we are ready to roll back the skin and cut through the muscular body wall to expose the internal organs. Study Figs. 64 and 65, and follow directions carefully. Directly under and attached to the body wall is a thin layer of tissue, a membrane called the *peritoneum* (see Fig. 68). This membrane forms a lining around all the abdominal organs and the body cavity or coelom. As you examine the internal organs you will see membranes that hold organs together. Still other membranes support the organs (see Figs. 67 and 68). Both types of membranes are called *mesenteries*. Each mesentery has a special name depending upon the organs with which it is associated. All the mesenteries are special parts of the peritoneum.

Fig. 66 shows the main organ systems and their arrangement in the male frog. The female frog differs basically from

Step 1. Using forceps lift skin as shown at point E and with scalpel cut skin free from F to D^1 and similarly from B to D. Pull skin back firmly with forceps as tip of scalpel cuts it free. The unattached spaces under skin are lymph spaces (important in circulation).

Step 2. Free the skin on both sides so as to expose the body wall. Roll all skin flaps back and pin each side to pan.

Step 3. Cut a small opening through muscular body wall at point C with scalpel or razor. Hold wall with forceps as you cut.

Step 4. Insert rounded tip of scissors into incision, holding scissors almost parallel to body. Continue cutting to point A where sternum (breastbone) begins. **Caution:** cuts must be very shallow or internal organs will be damaged. Now turn to Fig. 65.

Fig. 64. Opening Body Wall of the Frog.

the male frog only with respect to the presence of female reproductive structures. Study page 109, "The Urogenital (Excretory and Reproductive) Systems," before you begin to dissect the female frog.

In Fig. 66 the digestive organs have been moved aside so that you can see the structures of other systems. The liver sections or lobes are shown lifted and turned toward the head to reveal the gall bladder and its tubes, and the heart. Only one lung is shown but, of course, there is another lung on the other side of the heart. With probe and forceps move the parts of your specimen so that they are in the same positions as those shown in Fig. 66. Now locate each of the labeled parts.

Study Fig. 67 to get a more detailed idea of the anatomy and functions of the digestive system. It very closely resembles

103

Pectoral girdle.

Step 1. Cut body wall from point A to G and also from A to G^1.

Step 2. With forceps lift cut body wall AGG^1. It will form a triangular flap. Cut off the flap from point G to G^1.

Step 3. Using strong scissors cut through the bones (coracoid and clavicle) close to the joints at point G and G^1.

Step 4. Grasp and lift the sternum with forceps. Use scalpel to cut the pectoral girdle free from the body. This will expose the heart.

Step 5. Cut through body wall from point C to Y and then to D and D^1 as you did when the skin was cut.

Step 6. Pin back the cut body wall on both sides. Remove the thin peritoneal membrane with fine scissors if it was not removed with the cut body wall. We are now ready to study the internal organs.

Coracoid.

Clavicle.

Sternum.

Fig. 65. Cutting Through Body Wall and Pectoral Girdle of Frog to Expose Internal Organs.

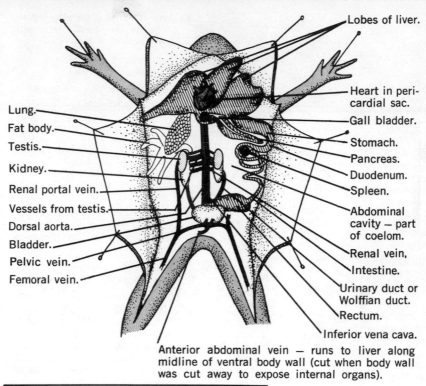

Lobes of liver.

Lung.

Fat body.

Testis.

Kidney.

Renal portal vein.

Vessels from testis.

Dorsal aorta.

Bladder.

Pelvic vein.

Femoral vein.

Heart in peri-
cardial sac.

Gall bladder.

Stomach.

Pancreas.

Duodenum.

Spleen.

Abdominal
cavity – part
of coelom.

Renal vein,

Intestine.

Urinary duct or
Wolffian duct.

Rectum.

Inferior vena cava.

Anterior abdominal vein – runs to liver along
midline of ventral body wall (cut when body wall
was cut away to expose internal organs).

Ventral view – left lung omitted to simplify
diagram; digestive system moved to one side.

Fig. 66. Internal Anatomy of Male Frog.

the pattern of your own digestive system. To see where the
esophagus originates, refer back to Fig. 61b.

Circulatory System

The circulatory system of the frog is very complicated
and, in many ways, resembles that of man. To understand it
we must study it in three divisions: 1) the heart with its
entrances and exits, 2) the system of main arteries and 3) the
system of main veins.

The heart is encased in a thin sac called the *pericardial
sac* (see Fig. 66). Cut through the thin membrane of this sac
with the tip of a very sharp razor. Do not cut the heart itself.
Then spread the membrane with forceps to expose the heart.
Now locate the parts of the heart as shown in Fig. 69. (This
is a ventral view. Other parts of the heart will be seen when

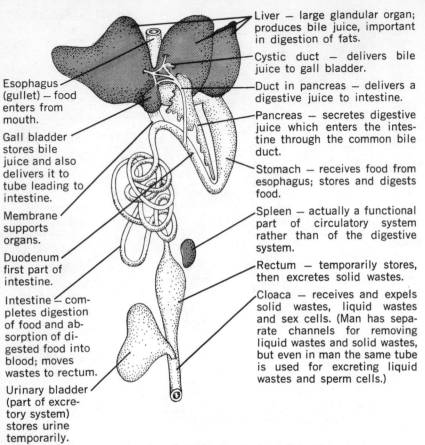

Esophagus (gullet) — food enters from mouth.

Gall bladder stores bile juice and also delivers it to tube leading to intestine.

Membrane supports organs.

Duodenum first part of intestine.

Intestine — completes digestion of food and absorption of digested food into blood; moves wastes to rectum.

Urinary bladder (part of excretory system) stores urine temporarily.

Liver — large glandular organ; produces bile juice, important in digestion of fats.

Cystic duct — delivers bile juice to gall bladder.

Duct in pancreas — delivers a digestive juice to intestine.

Pancreas — secretes digestive juice which enters the intestine through the common bile duct.

Stomach — receives food from esophagus; stores and digests food.

Spleen — actually a functional part of circulatory system rather than of the digestive system.

Rectum — temporarily stores, then excretes solid wastes.

Cloaca — receives and expels solid wastes, liquid wastes and sex cells. (Man has separate channels for removing liquid wastes and solid wastes, but even in man the same tube is used for excreting liquid wastes and sperm cells.)

Fig. 67. Digestive System of the Frog.

the heart is turned around for a dorsal view. See Fig. 71.) Study the arrows in Fig. 69, especially those in and near the heart. The blood vessels that carry blood away from the heart are arteries. Those that carry blood to the heart are veins. Notice that the *auricles* are fed by veins. The *ventricle* connects with one main vessel, the *truncus arteriosus,* which curves back toward the dorsal side and forms two loops around the esophagus and air tubes (see Fig. 70). These tubes are called the *systemic arches.* The two arches unite near the spine close to the stomach, and form a giant artery called the *dorsal aorta.* These two arches represent a primitive vertebrate condition. In humans only one systemic arch remains.

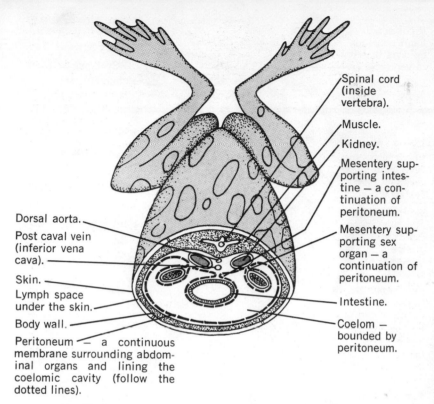

Dorsal aorta.

Post caval vein (inferior vena cava).

Skin.

Lymph space under the skin.

Body wall.

Peritoneum — a continuous membrane surrounding abdominal organs and lining the coelomic cavity (follow the dotted lines).

Spinal cord (inside vertebra).

Muscle.

Kidney.

Mesentery supporting intestine — a continuation of peritoneum.

Mesentery supporting sex organ — a continuation of peritoneum.

Intestine.

Coelom — bounded by peritoneum.

Fig. 68. Cross Section Through Abdomen of Frog Showing Position of Organs and Membranes.

Use probe and forceps to locate all the arteries shown in Fig. 69. A pen flashlight and a magnifying glass will be very helpful. Move the probe along each artery to see into which organ it goes. Once the arteries reach an organ they divide into smaller and smaller branches like the roots of a tree, until they form microscopic vessels called *capillaries*. The capillaries then run into larger vessels which finally emerge from the organs as veins. These veins carry blood toward larger veins (see Fig. 72) until they reach a part of the heart called the *sinus venosus* (see Fig. 71). Inside the sinus venosus is an opening to the right auricle. Through this opening passes the blood from all parts of the body except the lungs. The blood from the lungs returns to the heart directly into the left auricle. In man there is no sinus venosus but a small important thickening is present called the sinuaur-

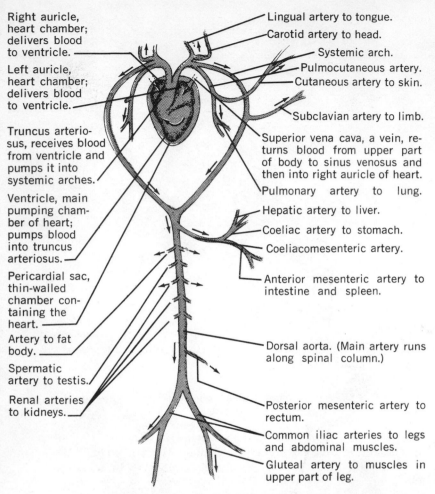

Right auricle, heart chamber; delivers blood to ventricle. ──

Left auricle, heart chamber; delivers blood to ventricle. ──

Truncus arteriosus, receives blood from ventricle and pumps it into systemic arches. ──

Ventricle, main pumping chamber of heart; pumps blood into truncus arteriosus. ──

Pericardial sac, thin-walled chamber containing the heart. ──

Artery to fat body. ──

Spermatic artery to testis. ──

Renal arteries to kidneys. ──

Lingual artery to tongue.
Carotid artery to head.
Systemic arch.
Pulmocutaneous artery.
Cutaneous artery to skin.

Subclavian artery to limb.

Superior vena cava, a vein, returns blood from upper part of body to sinus venosus and then into right auricle of heart.

Pulmonary artery to lung.

Hepatic artery to liver.
Coeliac artery to stomach.
Coeliacomesenteric artery.

Anterior mesenteric artery to intestine and spleen.

Dorsal aorta. (Main artery runs along spinal column.)

Posterior mesenteric artery to rectum.

Common iliac arteries to legs and abdominal muscles.

Gluteal artery to muscles in upper part of leg.

Fig. 69. Heart and Main Arteries of the Frog—Ventral View.

icular node which has an important job of helping to set the rhythm of the heartbeat. With Fig. 72 as a guide, trace all the main veins before you study the dorsal side of the heart.

Familiarize yourself with the location of the main veins and arteries of the heart. With Fig. 71 as a guide, remove the heart by snipping the following tubes with scissors: two branches of the *truncus arteriosus,* the two *superior vena cavae,* the *inferior vena cava,* the *pulmonary veins* and the *cardiac vein* (see Fig. 72). With fine scissors cut open the

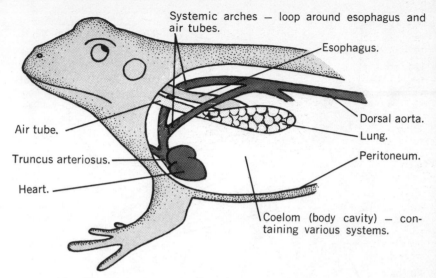

Systemic arches — loop around esophagus and air tubes.

Esophagus.

Dorsal aorta.

Air tube.

Lung.

Truncus arteriosus.

Peritoneum.

Heart.

Coelom (body cavity) — containing various systems.

Fig. 70. Aortic (Systemic) Arches of Frog—Side View.

sinus venosus at the level of the opening into the right auricle (see Fig. 71) and trace the opening into the right auricle. Use your probe to find out where each opening leads. With Fig. 69 as a guide, cut the auricles and ventricle open with a scalpel from the top of each down through the middle of each chamber, then examine the muscular walls of this amazing pump.

How the frog breathes while prudently keeping its mouth closed is explained in Fig. 73. The frog also breathes through its moist skin and through the membranes in its mouth. This is another reason why we find frogs living close to a source of water.

The Urogenital (Excretory and Reproductive) Systems

Fig. 74 shows the urogenital system of the female frog. During the breeding season the entire abdomen is swollen with eggs that cover most of the organs. To study the female reproductive organs it is necessary to first remove one ovary with its eggs before we dissect the female frog. Otherwise practically nothing can be seen. The ovary can be easily removed by opening the abdomen as shown in Figs. 64 and 65, lifting the masses of eggs with forceps, and snipping with scissors the membranes that hold the ovary in place. To study

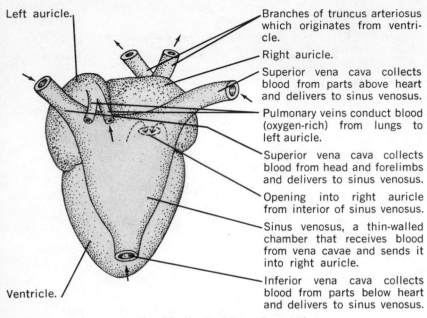

Left auricle.

Branches of truncus arteriosus which originates from ventricle.

Right auricle.

Superior vena cava collects blood from parts above heart and delivers to sinus venosus.

Pulmonary veins conduct blood (oxygen-rich) from lungs to left auricle.

Superior vena cava collects blood from head and forelimbs and delivers to sinus venosus.

Opening into right auricle from interior of sinus venosus.

Sinus venosus, a thin-walled chamber that receives blood from vena cavae and sends it into right auricle.

Inferior vena cava collects blood from parts below heart and delivers to sinus venosus.

Ventricle.

Fig. 71. Heart of Frog—Dorsal View.

all the internal organs, remove both ovaries. Once the ovaries are removed, the rest of the dissection is completed in the same manner as previously described in Figs. 64 and 65 for the male frog.

The male reproductive system is illustrated in Fig. 66. The male organs, the testes, produce sperm cells. These swim through tiny vessels by means of the action of a fin-like tail and migrate into the Wolffian duct or urinary duct. During the mating season the male frog tightly clasps the abdomen of the female with the aid of adhesive pads on the thumbs of his fore limbs. (See Fig. 60.) The male frog literally squeezes out the eggs from the female frog. The sperm move into the cloaca of the male frog and are then discharged over the eggs of the female frog, thus starting the life cycle anew. This clasping reflex is so overwhelmingly compelling in the male frog during the breeding season that—as proved by experiments—he will clasp a block of wood placed before him even after his head has been cut off.

In Charge—The Nervous System

The nervous system consists mainly of a brain located

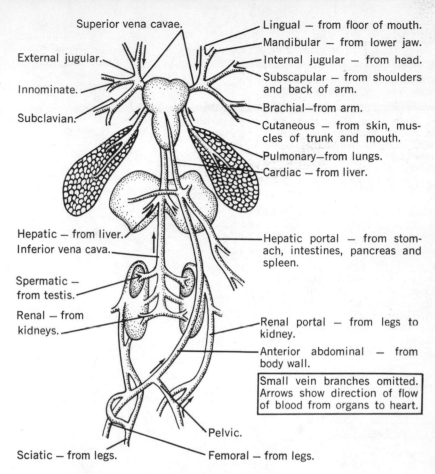

Superior vena cavae.

External jugular.

Innominate.

Subclavian.

Lingual — from floor of mouth.

Mandibular — from lower jaw.

Internal jugular — from head.

Subscapular — from shoulders and back of arm.

Brachial—from arm.

Cutaneous — from skin, muscles of trunk and mouth.

Pulmonary—from lungs.

Cardiac — from liver.

Hepatic — from liver.
Inferior vena cava.

Spermatic —
from testis.

Renal — from kidneys.

Hepatic portal — from stomach, intestines, pancreas and spleen.

Renal portal — from legs to kidney.

Anterior abdominal — from body wall.

Small vein branches omitted. Arrows show direction of flow of blood from organs to heart.

Pelvic.

Sciatic — from legs.

Femoral — from legs.

Fig. 72. System of Veins in Frog—Ventral View.

between the roof of the mouth and the surrounding bones in the dorsal part of the head (see Figs. 75, 76 and 77). Ten pairs of *cranial nerves* go from the brain to the eyes, tongue, other parts of the head and into the abdominal section. The brain is a concentrated mass of ganglia and nerves which connect with a spinal cord. The spinal cord is surrounded by the spinal column, consisting of bones called vertebrae. Ten pairs of spinal nerves reach all the parts of the body below the head. The combination of brain, spinal cord and nerves makes up the communications network that controls the behavior of the frog.

Since the main parts of the nervous system are in the

111

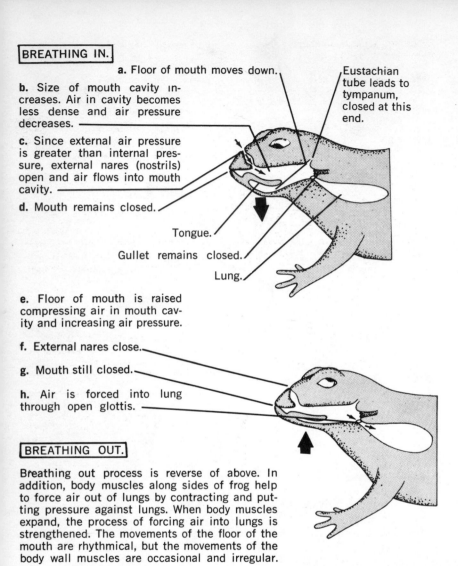

BREATHING IN.

a. Floor of mouth moves down.

b. Size of mouth cavity increases. Air in cavity becomes less dense and air pressure decreases.

c. Since external air pressure is greater than internal pressure, external nares (nostrils) open and air flows into mouth cavity.

d. Mouth remains closed.

Eustachian tube leads to tympanum, closed at this end.

Tongue.

Gullet remains closed.

Lung.

e. Floor of mouth is raised compressing air in mouth cavity and increasing air pressure.

f. External nares close.

g. Mouth still closed.

h. Air is forced into lung through open glottis.

BREATHING OUT.

Breathing out process is reverse of above. In addition, body muscles along sides of frog help to force air out of lungs by contracting and putting pressure against lungs. When body muscles expand, the process of forcing air into lungs is strengthened. The movements of the floor of the mouth are rhythmical, but the movements of the body wall muscles are occasional and irregular.

Fig. 73. How the Frog Breathes.

dorsal part of the frog the first thing we must do now is to turn the frog dorsal side up on the dissecting pan. The next step is to pin the frog to the pan and cut away the skin on each side of the spinal column. (See Fig. 75.) Use the same techniques in removing the skin and body wall from the dorsal

112

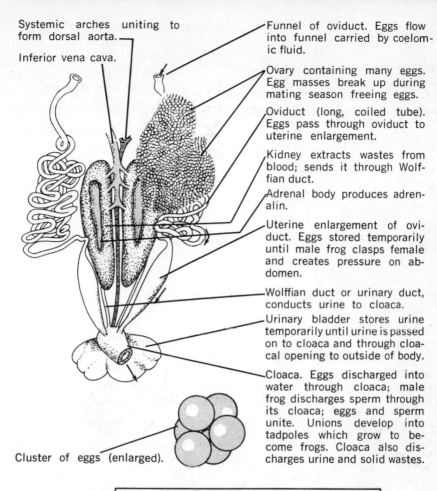

Systemic arches uniting to form dorsal aorta.

Inferior vena cava.

Funnel of oviduct. Eggs flow into funnel carried by coelomic fluid.

Ovary containing many eggs. Egg masses break up during mating season freeing eggs.

Oviduct (long, coiled tube). Eggs pass through oviduct to uterine enlargement.

Kidney extracts wastes from blood; sends it through Wolffian duct.

Adrenal body produces adrenalin.

Uterine enlargement of oviduct. Eggs stored temporarily until male frog clasps female and creates pressure on abdomen.

Wolffian duct or urinary duct, conducts urine to cloaca.

Urinary bladder stores urine temporarily until urine is passed on to cloaca and through cloacal opening to outside of body.

Cloaca. Eggs discharged into water through cloaca; male frog discharges sperm through its cloaca; eggs and sperm unite. Unions develop into tadpoles which grow to become frogs. Cloaca also discharges urine and solid wastes.

Cluster of eggs (enlarged).

Ventral view of urogenital system shown with egg masses omitted on one side to show structures below eggs.

Fig. 74. Diagram of Urogenital System of Female Frog During Breeding Season.

side as you did for removing the skin from the ventral side at the beginning of the dissection (see Fig. 64). Then cut through the body wall with scissors and remove the entire cut section of the body wall from tip of upper jaw to cloaca. Using forceps and scalpel to lift and cut, remove all tissue from the spinal bones leaving only the white tube-like nerves. These are the spinal nerves.

Eye.

Nostril.

Nasal capsule.
Fronto-parietal bone.
Auditory capsule.
Tympanum.
Cartilage behind cranium
(fronto-parietal bone).

Step 1. Lift cartilage with forceps.

Step 2. Insert tip of scalpel. Cut slightly upward and loosen cranium (fronto - parietal bones).

Step 3. With very fine small-tipped scissors cut through bones along dotted lines from the back of the head toward the front.

Step 4. Press the head gently together between two fingers (one finger at point A and the other at B). This will loosen skull bones.

Step 5. With forceps pick off fronto-parietal bone and adhering tissue. The brain is now exposed.

Fig. 75. Exposing the Brain and Spinal Column of the Frog—Dorsal View.

Now follow the directions on Fig. 75 for exposing the brain and spinal column. Be very careful to avoid injuring the brain and spinal nerves. When you have completed this, go on to Fig. 76 to dissect out the brain and spinal cord. Then identify the parts of the nervous system shown in Fig. 77.

We have completed a basic dissection of the frog. Now let's apply our knowledge in some experimental projects.

Project 1: Changing the Spots on a Leopard

We have all heard the expression "You can't change the

114

This section was removed in Fig. 75 to expose the brain.

Spinal cord.

Spinal process.

Step 1. Insert fine, but strong scissors tip on underside of neural arch. Do not damage spinal cord. Cut through neural arch of each vertebra.

Diagram below shows line of cut through neural arch of each vertebra.

Step 2. Bend spinal processes backward at point X and Y to loosen spinal cord. Repeat for each vertebra.

Step 3. Remove spinal cord and brain intact just snipping off adhering nerves to allow brain and spinal cord to come free.

Neural arch of vertebra.

Line of cut through neural arch.

Passageway for spinal cord.

Diagram of vertebra of frog.

Fig. 76. Removal of Brain and Spinal Cord from Frog.

spots on a leopard." Nobody expects you to try it. But we can change the spots on a leopard frog. This, however, should be done in school under supervision of a biology teacher.

Obtain two live pegged, small crabs or lobsters from a fish market and a live leopard frog from a biological supply house. With scalpel remove the eyestalks by cutting out a small ring of tissue where the eyestalks are attached to the head. Cut the eyestalk just below the eyes and discard the eyes. Grind the remaining tissue with a clean mortar and pestle. Add 5 cc of distilled water to the ground mixture and stir.

Filter the mixture (see page 54 for directions on filtering). Draw up the liquid in a sterilized 2 cc hypodermic syringe. The liquid now contains a hormone from the animal's sinus gland, the tissue you ground up. Rub the skin of the frog near

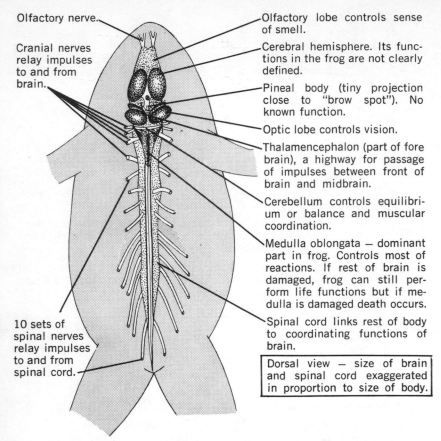

Olfactory nerve.

Cranial nerves relay impulses to and from brain.

Olfactory lobe controls sense of smell.

Cerebral hemisphere. Its functions in the frog are not clearly defined.

Pineal body (tiny projection close to "brow spot"). No known function.

Optic lobe controls vision.

Thalamencephalon (part of fore brain), a highway for passage of impulses between front of brain and midbrain.

Cerebellum controls equilibrium or balance and muscular coordination.

Medulla oblongata — dominant part in frog. Controls most of reactions. If rest of brain is damaged, frog can still perform life functions but if medulla is damaged death occurs.

10 sets of spinal nerves relay impulses to and from spinal cord.

Spinal cord links rest of body to coordinating functions of brain.

Dorsal view — size of brain and spinal cord exaggerated in proportion to size of body.

Fig. 77. Schematic Diagram of Frog's Central Nervous System.

the middle of its back with a piece of cotton saturated with alcohol. Lift the skin with forceps. Inject about ½ cc just under the skin of the frog. Do not penetrate the body wall. Try the same procedure on large tadpoles and on tropical fish larger than guppies. Clean the syringe with water and alcohol after use.

Keep the frog in a covered container with about one inch of water in it. Observe changes that take place during the first hour and check periodically for several hours. You will see some dramatic changes.

If you have used a lobster for this experiment, and if your family enjoys lobster cardinal, your experiment may end with a tasty snack on the dinner table.

Vagus nerve.

X

Ringer's (saline) solution.

Ring clamp.

Ring stand.

Tied tightly with fish line.

Overflow droplets containing acetylcholine from heart A.

Heart B's beat slows down.

Funnel.

A

B

Tie.

Fig. 78. Remote Control of Frog's Heartbeat.
Adapted from "Animal Physiology," by Knut Schmidt-Nielsen, ©
1960 by Prentice-Hall, Inc., Englewood Cliffs, N. J.

Project 2: Remote Control of a Frog's Heartbeat

Can stimulating a nerve connected with one heart cause the heart of another animal to change its beat? This was one of the truly great pioneer experiments by Otto Loewi on nerve transmission and the nature of a stimulus.

Study Figs. 69, 71 and 78 and carefully follow the directions for this project. Prepare 500 ml of Ringer's solution. A good book on animal physiology will list the ingredients of Ringer's solution. Dissect out the hearts of two live frogs, anaesthetized by keeping them for five minutes in a 5% water and urethane solution. Leopard frogs make good subjects. Cut the blood vessels as shown in Fig. 78. Be sure to leave about two inches of the vagus nerve attached to one of the hearts.

Using fish line tie one superior vena cava and the inferior vena cava of each of the two hearts. (See Figs. 69 and 71 to identify parts of heart and blood vessels.) Leave right superior vena cava open. Tie one branch of the systemic arch.

Attach funnels at appropriate levels to ring stands. Now insert each funnel end into each open superior vena cava. Tie each closed end of the systemic arch loosely to ring clamp to help support the hearts, as in Fig. 78. Then pour Ringer's solution into the top funnel. Wait until it begins to drip out of the open systemic arch.

To stimulate the vagus nerve, touch the cut end with a glass rod dipped in vinegar or acetic acid, or touch the vagus nerve with two ends of wires attached to a dry cell battery— watch the dramatic results! It is an exciting experiment which you can convert to an open-end experiment by adding an additional heart to the series or by adding at point X on Fig. 78 such chemicals as adrenalin, thyroxin, oxytocin, pitocin, barbiturates, aspirin, urethane and many others.

The frog is a member of a transitional vertebrate group, the Amphibia, from which emerged the Seymouria, called by some scientists an advanced amphibian and by others a primitive reptile. There followed a long geologic period during which reptiles advanced and flourished. From prehistoric reptiles belonging to the Thecodontia, the world of birds developed. From primitive reptiles the Pelycosauria gave rise to the Therapsida, reptiles which were similar to primitive mammals. The mammalian ascent which began with reptilian ancestry has moved into the present world, after an enormous span of time. Thus, the dissection of the frog illuminates not only a basis for understanding the anatomy of mammals such as the fetal pig and man, but highlights part of the stream of dynamic biological history.

We shall now turn our attention to the dissection of a mammal, the fetal pig.

The Fetal Pig—
Dissection of A Mammal.

DISSECTION is a way of discovery. *Macrodissection* enables the dissector to learn about gross anatomy. But what lies within the gross anatomy of a lung, a testis, an ovary or another organ? *Microanatomy* or *histology,* the study of tissues, and *cytology*, the study of cells, go on to a deeper level of discovery. A knowledge of anatomy is made more meaningful when it is coupled with an understanding of *physiology*, the science that tries to explain how an organism functions.

The domesticated pig is an important source of food for mankind. Some of its parts are used for other purposes that affect the lives of people. For example, some leather products are manufactured from the pig's skin. Our interest in the pig is focused on its excellence as a subject for dissection. However, for obvious reasons, we do not dissect an adult pig which is a relatively large and expensive animal. Fortunately, female pigs are very fertile. They breed readily and produce fetuses which, when allowed to develop, will emerge as new generations of pigs. This capacity enables the zoologist to obtain unborn but well developed fetuses that are very like in structure to the adult pig. There are some important differences, however, that will be noted later.

The fetal pig is an especially interesting specimen to dissect. Its dissection reveals relationships in structure with organisms lower in the evolutionary scale, like the frog for example, and enables you to examine the anatomy of a mammal whose internal parts are basically like the human anatomy. In fact, before starting this dissection it would be rewarding to review the anatomy of the frog (see Chapter 8) and to examine the human internal structure, illustrations of which are readily available in biology or anatomy textbooks.

119

Taxonomy Of The Pig

Every living thing has a name. There are international rules in the world of science for classifying and naming organisms. The rules belong to a branch of science called Taxonomy. You should consult a textbook for the study of the principles of taxonomy.

The name of an organism consists of its genus and its species. Note that the first letter of the *genus* is always capitalized in the name, but the first letter of the *species* is not capitalized.

The scientific name of the domesticated pig is *Sus scrofa*. We will indicate the main taxonomic groups to which the Sus scrofa belongs, beginning with the groups that include all of the progressively more limited groups.

The Pig in its Taxonomic Setting: The Main Groups

Phylum Chordata

    Animals with bilateral symmetry, evidences of segmentation developing from three germ layers or embryonic layers

    Presence of a coelom

    Single dorsal tubular nerve cord

    Gill slits in the pharynx

    A notochord (primitive supporting rod) present at some time in the life history of the organism

Group Craniata

    Chordates with a well defined head

Subphylum Vertebrata

    Craniates with a backbone

Superclass Tetrapoda

    Vertebrates with two pairs of limbs

Class Mammalia

    Tetrapods with hair, mammary glands and other common features

Subclass Theria

    Marsupial (bear young in a pouch) and placental mammals

Division Eutheria

    Mammals with a placenta

Order Artiodactyla

    Hoofed, herbivorous animals with an even number of digits on each toe (cloven hoofs)

Family Suidae

    Artiodactyls with four different types of teeth in each jaw, as well as other differentiating characters

Genus Sus
    Suidae that normally interbreed
Species scrofa
    The domesticated pig

Rationale For Fetal Pig Classification

The pig belongs to the Chordates because at some time during its life history from embryo to adult it has structures typically present in the Chordates. The basic features that link the Chordates are as follows:

The body is bilaterally symmetrical.
It is segmented.
There is a coelom present.
Each has a single tubular nerve cord.
The digestive system is fairly well developed.
There are paired gill slits in the pharynx.
A notochord, a cellular rod that helps to support the organs, is
    present.

The embryo pig has these conditions, but some become modified, reduced or lost as the pig develops.

The pig is a Craniate (a vertebrate tetrapod) because, like other vertebrates, it has the following structures (see Figure 80):

An internal endoskeleton, jointed skeleton, consisting of a *vertebral column (axial skeleton)* and a brain case (skull) or *cranium*. The axial skeleton ends in a tail.
Attached at joints to the axial skeleton are two groups of bones called girdles: the *pectoral girdle* forming the shoulder region and the *pelvic girdle* forming the hip region. To each of the girdles a pair of limbs or *appendages*, forelimbs and hind-limbs, respectively, are joined or articulated. The organism is therefore a *tetrapod*. The girdles and appendages make up the *appendicular skeleton*.
A system of muscles that attach to the bones by means of connective tissue enables the jointed skeleton to move. It also has a digestive system that has muscles.

121

The pig is a *mammal* because of the following characteristics:

1. hair
2. controlled body temperature
3. warmbloodedness
4. mammary glands for suckling its young
5. two pairs of limbs
6. differentiated teeth
7. a movable tongue
8. movable eyelids
9. ears with external pinnae
10. skin with several types of glands
11. seven neck vertebrae (cervical vertebrae)
12. two occipital condyles which joint the skull to the vertebral column
13. vocal cords
14. lungs
15. a muscular diaphragm that separates the thorax from the abdominal cavity
16. a completely four-chambered heart
17. mature red blood corpuscles of a non-nucleated nature
18. urinary bladder
19. penis for sexual mating
20. internal fertilization
21. pregnant pig has a placenta, and embryonic membranes form around the developing embryo
22. the brain has twelve pairs of cranial nerves

Therefore, the pig is a member of the Eutheria.

The pig is a chordate, vertebrate mammal included in the Order Artiodactyla. It belongs to this order chiefly because the third and fourth digits of each foot are about equal in structure, and a line divides these digits, forming the cloven hoofs. Thus the Artiodactyla is even-toed (Examples: camel, cattle and deer). Odd-toed hoofed mammals belong to the Perissodactyla.

Family Suidae

The pig and other members of this family have four well developed digits on each foot, with unfused metacarpal and metatarsal bones. The two outer digits on each foot do not reach the ground.

122

Another main reason for classifying the pig as a member of the Family Suidae is the four different kinds of teeth that are corresponding in the upper and lower jaws. This feature separates the pig from cattle, deer and camels, but enables the hippopotamus to be classified with the Family Suidae.

Genus and Species

The Sus scrofa is our target for dissection and study. We have placed the pig in its family and will begin to examine the specimen itself, after a look at the basic plan of its structure.

General Structure Of a Vertebrate

Figure 79 (page 124) is not a diagram of any real specific vertebrate. It does show the main parts of vertebrates in general and the approximate location of the parts as a vertebrate pattern. Of course an animal that is a lung breather will not have gill slits in its adult life. The converse is equally true.

No attempt has been made here to show the girdles or limbs. These will be examined later in relation to the pig's skeleton. Animals with a well developed vertebral column have only reduced notochordal remains. But the notochord is present during the early life of a vertebrate.

The basic framework or scaffolding of the tetrapod vertebrates, including the pig, is the internal skeleton which, except for the limbs and part of the skull, is entirely dorsally located. Much muscle under the skin or *integument* attaches to the skeleton. Other parts of the body such as the digestive organs and blood vessels also have considerable muscle tissue not connected with the skeleton.

The internal organs are located in cavities. The viscera, reproductive organs and excretory organs are in a large cavity called the *coelom* (see page 107, Fig. 68; Figs. 79 and 84, pages 123 and 130). The cloaca, a common receptacle for wastes and sex cells, becomes reduced and is replaced, becoming the channel for waste products and for sex cells, both eggs and sperm. Instead of the cloaca the adult pig has separate openings for the discharge of solid wastes and urine, with a more complex reproductive arrangement for effecting internal fertilization and development.

Before the actual dissection is begun it is important to bear in mind that the specimen is a fetus, not a fully developed pig. The

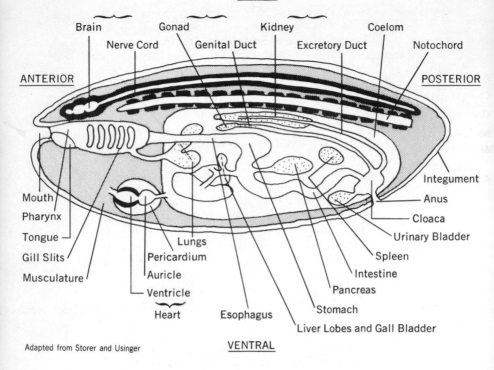

DORSAL

Brain · Gonad · Kidney · Coelom

Nerve Cord · Genital Duct · Excretory Duct · Notochord

ANTERIOR · POSTERIOR

Integument

Mouth · Anus

Pharynx · Cloaca

Tongue · Urinary Bladder

Lungs

Gill Slits · Pericardium · Spleen

Musculature · Auricle · Intestine

Ventricle · Pancreas

Heart · Esophagus · Stomach

Liver Lobes and Gall Bladder

Adapted from Storer and Usinger

VENTRAL

Fig. 79. A Generalized Plan of Vertebrate Anatomy: Sagittal View Showing Where Main Structures are Located.

specimen was removed from the placenta of a pregnant pig before birth. Thus there are some differences that are significant. The musculature of the fetal pig is difficult to dissect because the muscles are not clearly evident in their connections. In addition, the skeleton is still largely cartilaginous, not bony as in the adult. For these reasons we will not attempt to study the musculature in our dissection. However, we can utilize a diagram of the skeleton of a fetal pig and an actual skeleton of a cat and other mammalian skeletons that may be available in the laboratory. These will provide a satisfactory basis for understanding the mammalian skeleton, including man's, though there are differences in limb bones, vertebrae and skull.

124

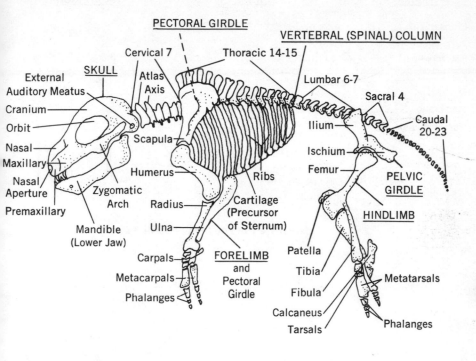

Fig. 80. Fetal Pig Skeleton.

The main structural sections of the fetal pig skeleton are shown in Figure 80. Here are diagrammed the two basic skeletal divisions: the *axial skeleton,* which consists of the skull and vertebral column and the *appendicular skeleton,* consisting of the pectoral girdle (shoulder bones), the articulated forelimbs, the pelvic girdle (hip bones) and the articulated hindlimbs. Note the even number of phalanges (digits) in each limb, characteristic of the Artiodactyla which includes pigs. Consider also how excellently the axial skeleton serves as a strong support for the weight and attachment of the muscles and internal organs which depend from the vertebral column. The vertebral column and its powerful muscles hold the heavy head, and the appendicular skeleton supports, by its muscular and connective tissue, the vertebral column.

Fig. 81. External View of Fetal Pig—Female Fetus.

Fig. 82. Ventral View of Male and Female Fetus—External Structures.

126

Since it is our prime object to serve as a guide for dissecting the fetal pig we recommend that students refer to a text dealing with the anatomy, histology, origin and physiology of bones and muscles for a better understanding of these tissues. It is now time to examine the actual specimen.

The External Anatomy—Getting Acquainted

The gestation period, the time it generally takes for the development to birth of a pig, is 112 days. Not all fetal pig specimens are of the same age; some are removed earlier or later than others. You can determine the approximate age of your specimen by measuring it with a millimeter ruler. At birth the pig is about 300mm long. Fetal pigs used for dissection vary in length. Pigs under 150mm are not desirable; they are rather small and young. A 220mm fetus is about 100 days old and is good for dissection. For comparison, a 40mm pig is about fifty-six days old, or about half way through its gestation period. Naturally, the rate of development is not uniform. It does accelerate as the pig gets older, since there are more cells which multiply in later periods of gestation than in earlier periods.

Place the specimen in a dissecting pan and rinse it in tap water to remove excess preservative which may be irritating to some people. Use Figures 81 and 82 to identify external parts. Determine the sex of your specimen.

Internal Anatomy—Preparing The Specimen for Dissection

Place the specimen ventral side up on a dissecting pan. Loop a string around a foreleg and another around a hindleg; then pass the strings under the pan to attach to the opposite legs, applying enough tension to stretch the legs apart, as shown in Figure 83. Gently and firmly pull the umbilical cord laterally to your left. Now, with forceps, grip the skin about 2cm directly anterior to the site of attachment of the umbilical cord to the body wall. Lift the skin and make an incision with a sharp scalpel, just long enough to insert the blunt end of dissecting scissors. (CAUTION: cut just deep enough to penetrate the body wall.) Insert scissor's end and carefully cut along median line (incision #1). Use a round end probe in side-to-side motions to disengage connective tissue as you progress with the scissors. With probe or your finger feel for

127

Fig. 83. Exposing the Internal Organs—Order of Incisions—Ventral Position for Dissection.

the first obstruction where the muscular diaphragm is attached to the ribs. Do not cut the ribs or diaphragm.

Carefully, as before, continue with scissors, now making two incisions, one on either side of the sternum, until you reach the tuft of hairs. Do not cut through the ribs at this point but peel away enough skin and other adhering tissue to see the surface of the ribs.

Now go on to incisions #2 and #3, using the same technique. Keep incision about 1cm to the right of the umbilical cord and similarly for incision #4, to the left of the cord. Before making incision #4 pull the umbilical cord outward to expose the umbilical vein which continues anteriorly from the cord. Cut and tie a small knot on the attached end of the umbilical veins for future reference and to enable you to fold back flaps #2, #3 and #4 towards the tail. Retain the severed piece of the umbilical cord for future study.

Start incision #5, after determining the position of the diaphragm with probe and fingers. Without damaging the diaphragm, free it from its connection to the rib cage on both sides of the median incision. Then start and complete incision #6. Be especially careful not to cut too deeply or the penis (if it is a male specimen) may be damaged. It is fairly close to the surface and posterior to the umbilical cord.

Now wash away the excess preservative and coagulated material from the inside of the body by running tap water gently over the exposed organs to prevent damaging them. Free the incised sections below the diaphragm and, with dissecting pins, pull each section laterally towards the sides of the pan and pin the flaps securely to the paraffin bed. This will expose the abdominal cavity, with its organs.

Digestive Organs in the Abdominal Cavity (see Figure 84)

A first view of the exposed visceral organs, the organs present in the abdominal cavity, reveal chiefly a glistening mass of coiled tubes—the intestines—capped by a large, dark red structure—the liver. Little else can be seen readily without manipulating the parts. The illustrations accompanying the text will show the structures in manipulated positions to emphasize the relationships of the various parts to each other. No individual parts should be severed unless so instructed or there will be damage, causing considerable difficulty in tracing the course of the circulatory system, as well as other connected structures. The student is cautioned to realize that neither anatomical illustrations nor actual photographs are perfect representations of the specimens. They are used as an aid to locating and studying the anatomy but cannot serve as a valid substitute for the real specimen which may have variations in size and position of parts with each specimen examined.

Heart

Thorax—showing position of lungs and heart

Lobes of Lungs

Pleural Cavity

Umbilical Vein

Muscular Diaphragm

Dissection Pin (on both sides)

Cut body wall pinned to pan

Coelom

Small Intestine

Continuation of Umbilical Vein

Allantoic Bladder

Umbilical Vein (cut–off–see above)

Allantoic Duct

Umbilical Cord

Umbilical Arteries

Urogenital Organ (Raised to show Rectum)   Urogenital Papilla

Pyloric Sphincter area of stomach connects with Duodenum, beginning of Small Intestine

Lobes of Liver (Raised to Show Gall Bladder)

Hepatic Duct

Gall Bladder and Cystic Duct

Stomach Pulled Posteriorly to Show Esophagus

Esophagus

Common Bile Duct— to Duodenum

Cardiac Sphincter Area of Stomach

Gastrosplenic Ligament

Spleen

Pancreas—its duct opens into Duodenum

Colon—Large Intestine

Caecum

Rectum (End of Colon)

Anus (End of Rectum)

Note: **Bold** first letter refers to a digestive organ. Other labels not so treated.

Fig. 84. Digestive Organs of the Abdominal Cavity— Ventral View. (Thorax exposed to show relationship with abdominal cavity—small intestine pulled to your left and large intestine to right—coils much reduced.)

Liver

The liver is a very large organ that has digestive and other functions. It is dark red, has several lobes or divisions and is located just posterior to the diaphragm. Raise the liver mass towards your left and locate the *gall bladder* and the *bile duct* which conducts previously stored bile juice from the gall bladder to the small intestine.

130

Stomach

The stomach is on the left side, below or dorsal to part of the liver. Pull the stomach slightly posteriorly to see its connection with the esophagus which extends from the base of the pharynx via the neck and thoracic cavity, emerging through the diaphragm to join the stomach at its cardiac end. The posterior end of the stomach is the *pylorus* where it is connected with the beginning of the small intestine. At each end of the stomach are ring-shaped muscles called *sphincters* (*cardiac* and *pyloric*) whose contractions control respectively the intake and expulsion of food.

Find the spleen, a narrow, red organ curved along the stomach. The spleen is hematopoietic (a blood cell forming organ), not a digestive structure. It is also a center for the elimination of blood cells.

Pancreas

The pancreas is below the stomach, i.e., dorsal and posterior to the stomach. It is light in color and looks somewhat like an irregular froth of bubbles called globules. The spleen, pancreas and stomach are held together by a strong, flexible membrane of connective tissue cells called a *mesentery*. Such membranes are the principal supporting and anchoring structures that hold the internal organs in place. They also provide a pathway for blood vessels.

Locate the *pancreatic duct* which leads from the pancreas to the first part of the small intestine called the duodenum.

The Intestines

The intestines are made up of two major parts: the *small intestine*, very long, very convoluted and rather narrow, and the *large intestine*, also convoluted but much shorter and wider. Both have strong involuntary muscles and digestive glands. The first part of the small intestine is the *duodenum*, a short tube into which the common bile duct and the pancreatic duct secrete their respective juices. The next part of the small intestine is a much longer section, the *jejunum*, followed by the *ileum*, also fairly long. However, in the pig the distinction between the jejunum and the ileum is vague. Near the end of the ileum is a pouch called the *caecum* which opens via the *ileo-caecal valve* into the large intestine, the *colon*. The last part of the colon is the *rectum* which finally ends in a muscular aperture called the *anus*, controlled by a *sphincter muscle*. The small intestine should be moved to the left and the large intestine to the right to see relationships. The intestines should not be removed or circulatory vessels will be destroyed. However, with much patience and care, using the fine, sharp point of a scalpel, you can clear away the epithelial and connective tissue, the mesenteric membranes, which hold the intestines together and support them. The blood vessels have been injected with colored latex by the supplier, the arteries red and the veins blue. The blood vessels are also ensheathed by the *mesenteries*. By carefully removing the mesenteries without cutting the blood vessels that interpenetrate the mesenteries, the course of blood in the viscera can be traced. It will also make it easier to locate the male or female urogenital system which lies mostly dorsal to the intestines.

The student should complement the dissection of each organ system with a review of the comparable system of the frog's anatomy and a study of the human's organ systems. Viewing dissected parts under a binocular stereomicroscope, and specimen tissue slides under a high power microscope, are highly recommended. In addition, each system should be diagrammed for better understanding of anatomical relationships and for retention of knowledge.

The Urogenital System (See Figure 85 for the Male Urogenital System and Figure 86 for the Female Urogenital System).

The urinary system and the genital system in both sexes have common receptacles and for that reason the two systems are treated together. It is advantageous at this stage for students to work in pairs, one with a male specimen and the other with a female specimen. Or, if this is not feasible, demonstration dissections showing the male and female urogenital systems should be available for examination.

Before starting the dissection of the urogenital system it would be helpful to look at an "anatomical road map" of its parts. Begin at the cut open end of the *umbilical cord*. There are four apertures. The latex dyes immediately proclaim the *umbilical* vein and the two *umbilical arteries*. The remaining aperture is the *allantoic duct*. This leads to the expanded section, the *allantoic bladder*. At the attached end of the umbilical cord are two tubes that join the posterior of the bladder, the *ureters*. At the end of the bladder is a broader tube, the *urethra*, which in the adult male pig continues into and through the *penis*. Its opening is posterior to the point of attachment of the umbilical cord to the body.

In the female the urethra opens directly into the *urogenital sinus*. In both the male and female pig the ureters meet the kidneys at the *hilum*, the site of the inward curve of the kidneys, and conduct liquid wastes from the kidneys to the urethra.

The male organs that produce sperm are the *testes*. In young fetal pigs the testes are in the abdominal cavity. In older ones and in the adult the testes have migrated into *scrotal sacs* on a connective tissue cord called the *gubernaculum* through two openings in the abdominal cavity, the *inguinal canals*. The sperm cells pass from each testis through the coiled *epididymis*, then through the sperm duct, and finally out through the urethra in the penis.

In the female are a pair of *ovaries* posterior to the kidneys. Coiled tubes (the *oviducts* or *Fallopian Tubes*) continue to the curved *horn of the uterus* on each side of the body. At the posterior end of the uterus is a constriction called the *cervix*, immediately below which is the *vagina*, which is joined by the *urethra* in a common receptacle called the *urogenital sinus*. The final aperture is the *urogenital pore* with its *urogenital papilla* and the *clitoris*.

Dissection of the Male Urogenital System

Move the small intestine to the left. Pin it to the dissecting pan so that it will not slip. Do the same with the colon on the right side. This helps to bring the *kidneys* into view. Spread the hind legs firmly apart but avoid excessive tension or the pelvic girdle will be disrupted. Locate the *penis* just below the ventral body wall and posterior to the umbilical cord. Free it carefully with probe and scalpel where needed and pick away fringe tissues with forceps. Trace it until you feel a hard substance. This is the *pelvic bone*. It meets with the *urethra* which empties into the *allantoic bladder*. In the adult, the allantoic bladder becomes the *urinary bladder*.

We will assume your specimen is not a young fetal pig whose testes would be in the abdominal cavity. The older ones have scrotal sacs into which the testes have migrated through the *inguinal canal*.

Now look for two tubes that come from the kidneys. These are the ureters. They are on either side of the rectum. There, locate two narrow tubes, the *sperm ducts*, that loop over the ureters and meet in front of the rectum. These enter two small bodies called *seminal vesicles*. Between the seminal vesicles is a small gland

133

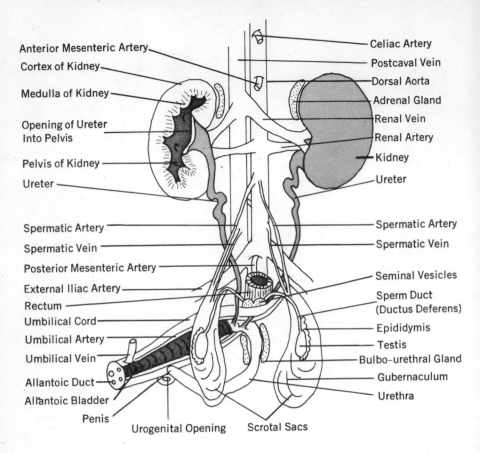

Anterior Mesenteric Artery

Cortex of Kidney

Medulla of Kidney

Opening of Ureter
Into Pelvis

Pelvis of Kidney

Ureter

Spermatic Artery

Spermatic Vein

Posterior Mesenteric Artery

External Iliac Artery

Rectum

Umbilical Cord

Umbilical Artery

Umbilical Vein

Allantoic Duct

Allantoic Bladder

Penis

Urogenital Opening

Scrotal Sacs

Celiac Artery

Postcaval Vein

Dorsal Aorta

Adrenal Gland

Renal Vein

Renal Artery

Kidney

Ureter

Spermatic Artery

Spermatic Vein

Seminal Vesicles

Sperm Duct
(Ductus Deferens)

Epididymis

Testis

Bulbo-urethral Gland

Gubernaculum

Urethra

Fig. 85. Urogenital System of Male.

called the *prostate gland*. Trace the sperm ducts back to their
origin, the testes. To see this it is necessary to cut through the *pubic
symphysis* where the pelvic girdle is fused laterally to the midline
of the girdle. First dissect away the tissues of the body wall.
Beneath this there are muscles which must be removed until you
can see a pale line. Touch this to confirm its hardness. This is the
pubic symphysis. With the point of a sharp scalpel pierce the line
to divide the girdle. DO NOT CUT DEEPLY.

It is necessary to cut open the inguinal canal to follow the
sperm ducts into the scrotal sacs which also should be slit open.
Find the epididymis, a tightly coiled mass on the surface of each
testis. Each sperm duct is a continuation of the epididymis. The

Anterior Mesenteric Artery	Dorsal Aorta
Post Caval Vein	Adrenal Gland
Renal Artery	Left Ovarian Vein
Renal Vein	Renal Artery
Renal Artery	Kidney
	Ureter
Right Ovarian Vein	Rectum
Right Ovarian Artery	
	Ovary
Ureter	Fallopian Tube
Umbilical Artery	Horn of Uterus
Ureter to Bladder	Uterus
Allantoic Bladder	Cervix
Umbilical Vein	Vagina
Urethra	Urogenital Sinus
	Clitoris
	Genital Papilla
Umbilical Artery	Anus
Allantoic Duct	
Umbilical Cord Cut to Show Interior	

Fig. 86. Urogenital System of Female.

sperm cells produced by the testes pass through the epididymis, the sperm ducts, the seminal vesicles and the urethral part of the penis to effect internal fertilization. Finally, locate the paired *spermatic arteries and veins* that lead into the scrotal sacs.

Dissection of the Female Urogenital System

Identify the bean-shaped kidneys. At the apex of each kidney is an *adrenal gland*, an endocrine gland of great physiological importance but not a urogenital organ. A little caudad (towards the tail) of the kidneys are the *ovaries*, light colored, egg shaped structures bounded by a fringe of tiny tubules, the *Fallopian tubes*. From the ovary trace the Fallopian tubes to the horns and

135

body of the *uterus*. Continue identification of the *cervix* and *vagina*. As explained previously, the vagina and urethra join to form the *urogenital sinus*.

Repeat the procedure for cutting the pubic symphysis, as explained above. Find the confluence of the vagina and the urethra. This is where the urogenital sinus begins. Trace the sinus to the *urogenital pore*, the *urogenital papilla and the clitoris* just below it.

Dissection of the Renal Part of the Urogenital System

While dissecting the genital system of the male and female fetal pig, several of the urinary structures were observed and their association with the genital systems were noted. We can therefore start with the ureters. Find the place where the ureters connect with the inward curve of the kidneys. Strip away the *peritoneal membrane* from one kidney and free it, without cutting the connecting blood vessels. Identify the *renal veins* coming from the *postcaval vein* and the *renal arteries* arising from the *dorsal aorta*, which is alongside the postcaval vein.

Carefully slice the kidney sagitally, that is, a longitudinal and equal split along the middle plane (like separating the two halves of a peanut). With a hand lens or a binocular microscope, observe the open spaces in the sliced kidney halves. These spaces, called the *pelvis*, form a continuous drainage system from the *renal tubules* to the *ureters* and successively to the *bladder, urethra, urogenital sinus* and *urogenital pore*. Although it is not sharply clear in the fetal condition, you may observe that the kidneys have two distinct areas, the inner dark area called the *medulla* and a lighter section around the medulla called the *cortex*, with its tubules and rich blood supply.

Examining the Internal Anatomy of the Thorax (See Figures 87 and 90)

Complete incision #7 using bone scissors (see Fig. 83, page 128) to cut through the ribs on both sides of the *thorax*. Be careful not to cut too deeply or you may damage the lungs and heart. Remove the cut sections to expose the *pleural lining* of the lungs and the *pericardial sac* encasing the heart. The *diaphragm* was freed when you performed incision #5.

Locate the lobed *lungs*, the *heart* and part of the *thymus*. The cavity which is almost obliterated by the lungs and heart is the

136

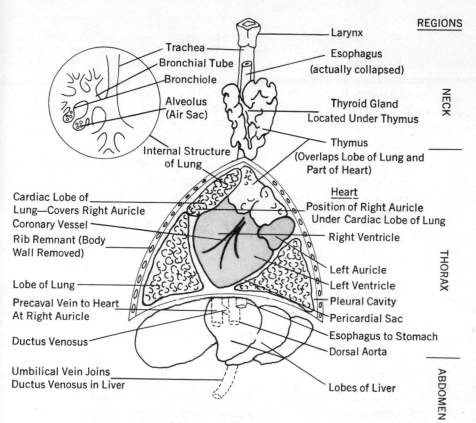

Larynx

Trachea
Bronchial Tube
Bronchiole

Esophagus
(actually collapsed)

Alveolus
(Air Sac)

Thyroid Gland
Located Under Thymus

Internal Structure
of Lung

Thymus
(Overlaps Lobe of Lung and
Part of Heart)

Heart

Cardiac Lobe of
Lung—Covers Right Auricle
Coronary Vessel
Rib Remnant (Body
Wall Removed)

Position of Right Auricle
Under Cardiac Lobe of Lung

Right Ventricle

Lobe of Lung

Left Auricle
Left Ventricle

Precaval Vein to Heart
At Right Auricle

Pleural Cavity
Pericardial Sac

Ductus Venosus

Esophagus to Stomach
Dorsal Aorta

Umbilical Vein Joins
Ductus Venosus in Liver

Lobes of Liver

Fig. 87. Organs of Respiratory System in Thorax and Neck.
(Ventral View—Other organs represented to show relative positions.)

thoracic cavity. It is part of the larger cavity called the *coelom.* The organs posterior to the diaphragm are in the *abdominal coelom,* the *peritoneal cavity,* while the heart and lungs are in the *thoracic coelom,* all of which are lined with *epithelial cells.*

There are actually three divisions of the coelom in the thorax. Between the left and right lung the heart lies in its *pericardial cavity.* In turn, the pericardial cavity, thymus, part of the dorsal aorta and the precaval vein are in the *mediastinal cavity,* which is almost completely filled space. It extends medially from the sternum and dorsally to the vertebral column, containing blood vessels, the trachea, esophagus and the pericardial sac.

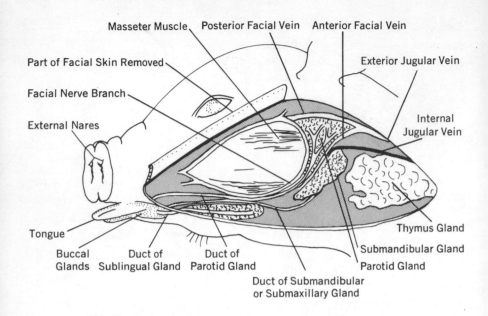

Masseter Muscle   Posterior Facial Vein   Anterior Facial Vein

Part of Facial Skin Removed

Facial Nerve Branch

External Nares

Exterior Jugular Vein

Internal Jugular Vein

Tongue

Thymus Gland

Buccal Glands   Duct of Sublingual Gland   Duct of Parotid Gland

Submandibular Gland

Parotid Gland

Duct of Submandibular or Submaxillary Gland

Fig. 88. Superficial Structures of Face—Lateral View.

Pull and lift the left lung to see the dorsal aorta, esophagus and the *phrenic nerves* which serve the diaphragm. The internal structure of the lungs with the arborization of the *bronchial tubes* leading to the microscopic *air sacs* or *alveoli* can best be seen in specially prepared sections for microscopic examination.

Delicately cut open the thin *pericardial membrane* around the heart, preparatory to a study of the circulatory system. This sequence will enable you to see the connections between the pre-thoracic and post-thoracic parts of the digestive, respiratory and circulatory systems. However, before going forward with the dissection of the circulatory system we will dissect part of the head and neck.

Internal Structures of the Head and Neck (See Figure 88)

Starting at the upper jaw near the proximal end of the snout (the end attached to the body), cut through the skin towards the ear and below the eye. Continue the incision to the neck and back, and forward to the base of the snout. Remove the skin to expose

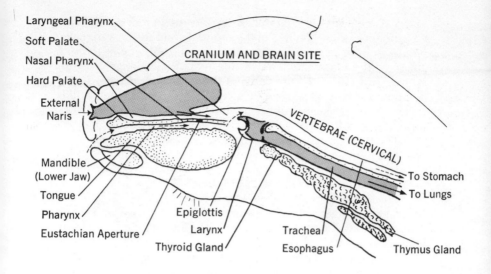

Fig. 89. Sagittal Section of Head—Showing Respiratory Channels (Solid Arrows) and Digestive Channels (Dashed Arrows).

superficial structures. Curving over and around a large muscular mass called the *masseter* are branches of the *facial nerve*. The nerve is white. Along the posterior curve of the facial nerve is the large reddish *parotid gland*, one of the *salivary glands*. Trace the *parotid duct* from the gland ventrally and below the masseter to the mouth. Below the parotid is another salivary gland, the *submandibular* or *submaxillary gland*. Its duct opens to the floor of the mouth. Another salivary gland, the *sublingual*, lies forward and ventral to the submandibular gland. Its duct, which is difficult to trace, also opens into the floor of the mouth. Flanking the parotid gland are the branches of the *facial vein* which arise from the *external jugular vein*. The *internal jugular* may be seen near the thymus gland.

Investigating the Interior of the Mouth and Pharynx (See Figure 89)

Use the upper surface of the tongue as a guide for freeing the upper jaw from the lower jaw. With scissors cut through the

139

external wall, laterally. Gradually spread the mouth open. With your finger explore the roof of the mouth to feel the forward *hard palate* and the posterior *soft palate*. Beyond the end of the soft palate is the *epiglottis*, a valve-like flap at the opening of the *larynx*. Just above the epiglottis at the *laryngeal pharynx* is the beginning of the *esophagus*, which you previously met in the thorax. The esophagus connects with the stomach, after it penetrates the diaphragm.

The main structures of the digestive organs in the mouth are lips, teeth, tongue, jaws, pharynx, hard and soft palates, salivary glands and esophagus. The adult pig has four types of teeth: *incisors, canines, premolars* and *molars*.

The dental formula of the fetal pig is written as I_7^3, C_1^1, P_4^4, and M_0^0. The fractions refer to the teeth of the upper jaw and lower jaw. Since the molars do not appear in the fetal pig the formula for fetal molars is M_0^0.

Your specimen probably has some erupted incisors. Remove one from the lower jaw for examination.

The Circulatory System (Study Figures 90 through 96)

A living organism, plant or animal, unicellular or multicellular, is dependent upon its external environment for life sustaining chemicals and sources of direct or auxiliary energy. All parts of the organism selectively utilize these needed chemicals. So it is that even in microscopic unicellular organisms a mode of transport is evident. Whether is is by a constant streaming of protoplasm or a network of minute canals, the distribution of chemicals is accomplished and the organism lives. In multicellular life an internal transport system is highly organized and structuralized. Such a system requires a flowing medium, the blood and the lymph. A propelling structure, the heart, with its muscular tissue, a closed circuit of tubes, arteries and veins and an interconnecting network of fine vessels, the capillaries, all serve the cells of the body. Thus the blood and lymph, in "making the rounds," manage to service all the cells of the organism unless a blockage occurs, caused either by disease or accident. The circulatory system is therefore not merely a pump with tubes attached; it is alive and its function goes beyond mechanical transport. Blood and lymph are also major factors in combatting disease and in temperature control.

Let us now examine the circulatory system of the fetal pig and see how it differs from the circulatory system of the adult pig.

The Paths of Blood in the Fetal Pig—Placenta to Placenta

It is important to remember that the fetal circulation starts with the fetal placenta. While soluble food and oxygen pass from the maternal placenta into the blood stream of the fetus, fetal blood and fetal blood cells do not. They are independently formed and remain within the circulatory system of the fetus. The structural circulatory system of the fetus is "weaned away" from the mother, starting with its first breath and producing several changes associated with the development of the lungs as the new respiratory mechanism. When the fetus is born the umbilical "lifeline" is parted from the mother and an independent life system is ready for growth.

Let us first examine the main paths of the fetal plan of circulation and then see how it differs from the adult circulation.

The Placenta to Placenta Circuit

1. Oxygen and food-rich blood from the *fetal placenta* pass through the *umbilical vein*.
2. The blood continues to the *ductus venosus* at the liver, connecting with the *postcaval vein*. Some blood is diverted through *liver sinuses* into the *hepatic veins* which also join the postcaval vein.
3. Blood continues to the *right atrium* of the heart, through the *foramen ovale* (an aperture between the right and left atria) and into the *left atrium*. The foramen ovale serves as a pulmonary bypass.
4. From the left atrium the blood is forced into the *left ventricle*.
5. The blood, still enriched, is then pumped into the aorta and via arterial branches to the head, shoulder and forelimbs—*not* to the lungs.
6. Veins conduct blood with diminished oxygen from the head and forelimbs through the precaval vein to the right atrium.
7. From the right atrium the blood moves into the *right ventricle*.
8. The right ventricle drives blood into *pulmonary arteries* to the lungs and, via the *ductus arteriosus*, into the *decending aorta*; then to the hindlimbs and visceral organs (See Fig. 93, page 154).

141

9. Finally, deoxygenated blood returns to the *placenta* through the paired *umbilical arteries* carrying metabolic wastes, to renew the food and oxygen supply and to remove cellular wastes.

The Adult Circulation—Heart to Heart

1. The right division of the heart may be considered the beginning of the blood circuit. The *right atrium* receives deoxygenated blood from the *precaval vein* and the *postcaval vein* (See Figures 90 and 91, pages 144-145).
2. Blood is propelled into the *right ventricle*. The *foramen ovale* is closed, preventing passage of blood from the right atrium to the left atrium.
3. The *right ventricle* pumps blood into the lungs via the *pulmonary arteries*. No blood enters the *ductus arteriosus* because that vessel becomes a closed cord after birth.
4. The blood is oxygenated in the lungs, returning to the left atrium of the heart through the *pulmonary veins*. This is the first of two major heart-to-heart circuits, the *pulmonary circuit* and the *systemic circuit*.
5. From the left atrium blood is forced into the left ventricle, which has powerful cardiac muscles.
6. The contractions of the left ventricle create a strong propulsive action that drives the oxygenated blood to all the rest of the body, excluding the lungs. Part of the original placental circuit becomes converted into non-conducting structures; the *ductus venosus*, the *umbilical vein* and the *umbilical arteries* remain as *ligaments*.
7. Blood is returned from the capillaries all over the body, excluding the lungs, which by successive confluences form ever larger tributary veins, ultimately leading into the very large precaval and postcaval veins. The caval veins deliver deoxygenated blood to the right atrium from the rest of the non-respiratory parts of the body. This begins the second major heart-to-heart circuit, the *systemic circuit*.

Tracking the Venous Circulation (See Figures 90 and 91)

A logical place to start is at the heart. You have already partially removed the pericardial membrane exposing the ventral surface of the heart. Using Figure 90 as a reference source, locate the right and left *auricles*, flap-like structures covering the right and left *atria* or chambers which are at the anterior end of the heart. Posterior to the auricles are the right and left *ventricles*. Bear in mind that the pig is on its back so that its left side faces your right side. Observe the large vessel that descends to meet the right auricle. This is the *precava* or precaval vein.

We will temporarily postpone dissection of the heart until we have tracked the main venous and arterial vessels. It is important to remember that the venous system in the fetal pig cannot be represented by a fixed blueprint. Some of the vessels may not appear individually but are joined with others, and are not always found at the expected position. However, it is still possible to locate the main veins and arteries, particularly since they are well color coded, red for arteries and blue for veins.

Patiently clear away tissue from the precaval vein and its anterior and lateral branches. Remove most of the thymus gland and thyroid gland. Slide the probe under and along blood vessels to free them. Muscle masses should be raised, freed and removed, always being watchful not to injure the larger blood vessels and nerves which look like light nylon strands.

The first branch you will meet, moving anteriorly, is on the left side. It is the *costocervical trunk*. Find its three branches, *dorsal, deep cervical* and *vertebral*. Some of the *intercostal veins* from the thorax also return blood to the costocervical trunk.

The precaval vein divides to form two short trunks called the *innominate veins*. Branches fan out from the innominates on the right and left sides. The main ones, in addition to the costocervical veins shown in Figure 90 are drawn somewhat extended to enable the dissector to see more readily the sequence of branches of the precaval vein.

Referring to Table I. Part 1., find these paired veins in the following order:

1. Costocervical trunk
2. Internal mammary
3. Subclavian and its continuations, Axillary and Brachial
4. Subscapular
5. Internal jugular
6. External jugular

Now go on to the dissection of the veins posterior to the heart. (Refer to Table I, Part 2, and to Figure 91).

143

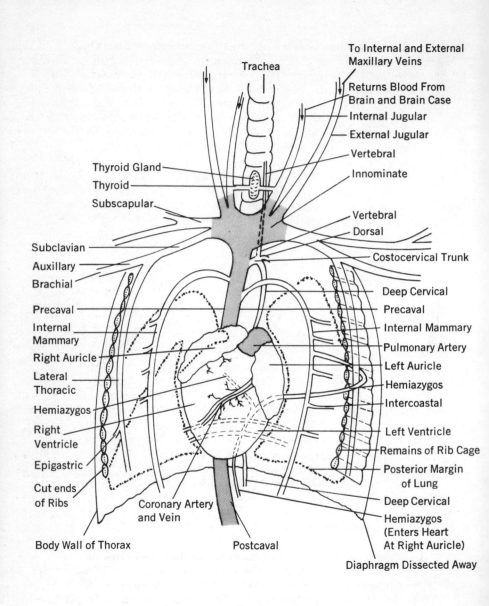

Fig. 90. The Anterior Venous Vessels—The Precaval "Tree"—Ventral View.

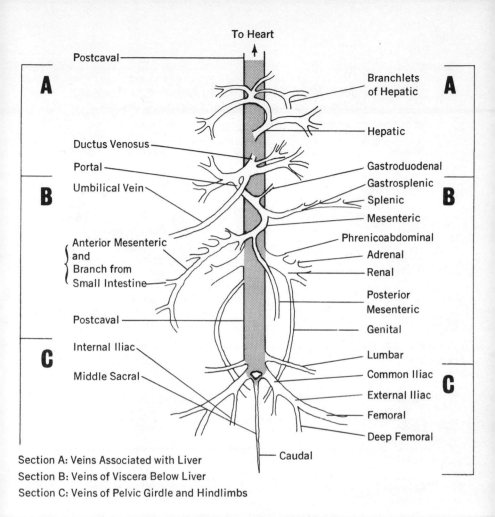

To Heart

Postcaval

A

Branchlets of Hepatic

A

Hepatic

Ductus Venosus

Portal

Umbilical Vein

B

Gastroduodenal

Gastrosplenic

Splenic

Mesenteric

B

Anterior Mesenteric and Branch from Small Intestine

Phrenicoabdominal

Adrenal

Renal

Posterior Mesenteric

Postcaval

Genital

C

Internal Iliac

Middle Sacral

Lumbar

Common Iliac

External Iliac

Femoral

Deep Femoral

C

Caudal

Section A: Veins Associated with Liver
Section B: Veins of Viscera Below Liver
Section C: Veins of Pelvic Girdle and Hindlimbs

Fig. 91. The Posterior Venous Vessels—The Postcaval "Tree".

Manipulate organs by lifting or moving them to the side in order to find veins which are not otherwise readily observable. Do the same when locating and identifying the arteries. Slice through and pick away membranes surrounding the blood vessels. Dissection of the heart will follow investigation of the arterial system.

Table I. Part 1. Main Veins Arising Anterior to the Heart (With Heart as the Ultimate Reference Point)

VEINS	ASSOCIATED WITH	PARTS OF BODY SERVED
Precava (Anterior Vena Cava or Superior Vena Cava)	Right atrium of heart	Receives blood from vessels serving head, pectoral area, forelimbs and part of thorax.
Costocervical Trunk	Precava	Receives blood from Vertebral, Deep Cervical, Dorsal and Subcostal veins.
Internal Mammary	Precava	Conveys blood from ventral ribs along ventral body wall.
Internal Thoracic	Precava	Drains blood from anterior abdominal area and from some ventral Intercostal veins.
Innominate	Precava	Short bifurcations of Precava. Returns blood to Precava.
Subclavian	Innominate	Carries blood returning from forelimbs.
Lateral Thoracic	Subclavian	Muscles of thoracic wall (mainly).
Subscapular	Near union of Axillary and Subclavian.	Shoulder
External Jugular	Innominate near heart and union of Internal and External Maxillary veins, anteriorly.	Mainly muscles and other tissues of head.
Internal Jugular	Innominate	Cranium and brain
Hemiazygos (single vein)	Right Auricle	Transports blood from intercostal cells, cells surrounding and between the ribs, to the heart.
Pulmonary	From lungs to Left Atrium. To locate these veins trace from left lung to heart.	Returns blood from lungs to heart.

146

Table I. Part 2. Main Veins of the Postcaval Route (With Heart as the Ultimate Reference Point)

VEINS	ASSOCIATED WITH	PARTS OF BODY SERVED
Postcaval (Posterior or Inferior Vena Cava)	Right Atrium	Traverses length of body posteriorly from pelvic area to right atrium. Collects & transports blood from its tributaries.
Veins of Hepatic Portal Sub-Route	Veins from Liver to Postcaval. Union of Gastrosplenic and Mesenteric veins.	Deliver blood from liver to Postcaval; carries blood from digestive organs to liver sinuses.
Hepatic	Several veins that arise from extensive liver capillaries & blood sinuses & empty into Postcaval.	Forms anterior path to Postcaval starting with Portal vein.
Umbilical	From umbilical cord to Ductus Venosus, a wide tube emptying into the Postcaval.	Conducts blood from placenta to Postcaval.
Renal	From Kidneys, singly or possibly doubly. Runs into Postcaval.	Carries blood from kidneys to Postcaval.
Adrenal	From Adrenal usually directly to Postcaval. Sometimes one runs into Renal vein.	Adrenal glands
Genital	Enter Postcaval caudad to Renals (Internal Spermatic in male & Utero-ovarian in female). Left Internal Spermatic may join left Renal.	Delivers blood from gonads to Postcaval.
Anterior Mesenteric	From small intestine joins Mesenteric.	Distributes blood from small intestine to Mesenteric vein.
Gastrosplenic	Mesenteric	Stomach and spleen
Splenic	Mesenteric	Spleen
Mesenteric	Combines with Gastrosplenic and connects to form Portal vein.	Carries blood from stomach, spleen and intestines to Portal vein.
Posterior Mesenteric	Runs into Mesenteric.	Blood moves from colon (large intestine) to Mesenteric vein.

147

Table I, Part 2 (Cont'd.)

Lumbar	Postcaval (chiefly)	Returns blood from dorsal interior cells of lumbar region.
Common Iliac	Begins at terminal bifurcation of Postcaval.	Directs blood from pelvic area & hindlimbs to Postcaval vein.
External Iliac	Main tributary of Common Iliac.	Delivers blood to Common Iliacs from pelvic area & hindlimbs.
Middle Sacral	Thin prolongation of Postcaval.	Serves tissues in sacral region.
Caudal	Prolongation of Middle Sacral	Carries blood from tail to Middle Sacral.

The Arterial System—Some Basic Facts to Remember

Arteries are muscular and help the heart's driving action. They conduct blood away from the heart and towards the biological consumers, the *cells* of the body, by way of the middleman, the capillaries. Another circulatory middleman is the *lymphatic system*. Unlike the circulatory system which is a *closed vascular system*, the lymphatic system begins with open *tissue spaces*. These connect with *lymph capillaries* which, in turn, run into larger vessels called *lymphatic ducts*. The *ducts* pass through *lymph nodes*, centers for the production of lymphocytes, on the way to the heart. Protection against bacterial infections of the transport system occurs in the lymph nodes by the action of phagocytes which collect in the nodes. They engulf the infective agents.

As blood moves through the capillaries it yields soluble nutrients, oxygen and other metabolites to the lymph spaces, forming lymph. The lymph diffuses the metabolites to the cells and takes up cellular products such as urea, carbon dioxide and other substances. An interchange between the blood-lymph-cells combination goes on continuously. The flow of lymph is towards the heart. We should know however that, among other functions, the lymphatics act as a kind of drainage apparatus serving the closed circuit systems of arteries, capillaries and veins.

148

Sequence represents arterial connections mainly from cephalic to caudal axis for Abdominal Aorta and reverse for Aortic Arch.

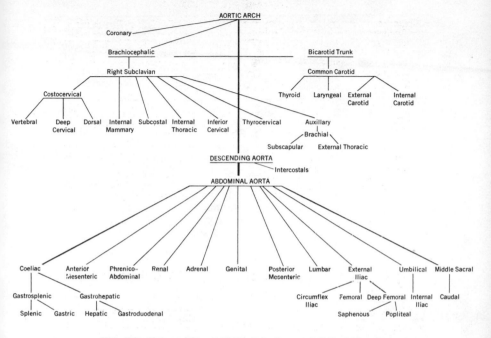

Fig. 92. Schematic of Main Arteries and Tributaries on Right Side Exclusive of Pulmonary Circuit.

The veins return the changed (deoxygenated) blood content to the heart, which rhythmically provides the initial force to keep the blood flowing. The venous system has two major vessels, *Precava* and *Postcava*, comparable in size to the main single artery called the *Aorta*.

Just as the venous system can be functionally treated in sub-divisions such as the *Hepatic Portal Circuit* and the *Systemic Circuit*, so can the arterial system be considered. Study Table II, Part 1 preparatory to dissection of the arteries. There you will find two subdivisions, the *Pulmonary Circuit* and the *Systemic Circuit*.

Begin with the *Pulmonary Circuit*. Use Table II and Figures 93 through 96 (pages 154-157) as a guide to trace the course of the arteries from the heart. Starting at the heart, clear away tissue to expose the paths to the arteries. Continue to do the same for the dissection of the *Systemic Circuit*.

Table II. Part 1. The Arterial Delivery System: Main Routes (The Pulmonary Circuit)

ARTERIES	CONNECTIONS	BLOOD DELIVERED TO
Pulmonary	Right ventricle with dichotomy forming left and right pulmonary artery branches, one to each lung.	Lungs. Blood returned by pulmonary veins to left auricle.
Ductus Arteriosus	A blood shunt between pulmonary artery and aorta at arch of aorta. At birth the lumen of the ductus arteriosus closes to become the ligamentum arteriosum. A dangerous congenital anomaly is sometimes found in human babies resulting from retention of open ductus arteriosum.	Fetal pig: blood is short-circuited from right ventricle into aorta. A lesser volume of blood goes into pulmonary arteries to lungs. In the adult: all the blood flows from right ventricle via pulmonary artery directly to the lungs.

Table II. Part 2. The Arterial Delivery System (The Systemic Circuit)

ARTERIES	CONNECTIONS	BLOOD DELIVERED TO
Aorta (Ascending)	From Left Ventricle	Aids in forcing blood beyond Left Ventricle
Aortic Arch	Aorta curves over anterior ventral part of heart to descend dorsally near vertebral column with branches to all parts of body except lungs (see Ductus Arteriosus).	Branches going to head, neck, forelimbs & thorax
Tributaries of Aortic Arch Coronary Arteries	Right & Left Coronaries arise from Aorta. Right is dorsal & left lies obliquely along ventral side of heart. Right Coronary joins Hemiazygos.	Heart cells
Brachiocephalic	Branches into the Bicarotic Trunk or into two separate Common Carotids & Right Subclavian.	Anterior part of body from thorax to head, via its branches

Table II, Part 2 (Cont'd.)

Left Subclavian	Arises directly from Aortic Arch. (Right Subclavian arises from Brachiocephalic).	Delivers blood to branch arteries of thorax, left forelimb, neck & head.
Tributaries of Brachiocephalic	Either divides into Common Carotids or Carotids may arise independently.	(See Bicarotid Trunk below)
Right Subclavian	Continues to forelimb as Brachial Artery with several branches, before becoming Brachial.	Note: Arterial branches of Left Subclavian parallel those of Right Subclavian
Branches of Subclavian		
Costocervical Trunk	Divides into 3 branches.	(See below)
Vertebral		Cervical vertebrae & skull
Deep Cervical	Forms First Intercostal.	Dorsal muscles of part of neck
Dorsal		Interior muscles of upper part of back & dorsal muscles of lower part of neck
Internal Mammary	Subclavian	Mammary glands, Thymus & some Pectoral muscles
Subcostal	Subclavian	Several Intercostals
Internal Thoracic	Subclavian—also branches to the Superior Epigastric.	Ventral Intercostals & parts of upper abdomen
Inferior Cervical	Subclavian, before it becomes the Brachial.	Sides of neck & proximal part of shoulder
Thyro-Cervical	Left Subclavian near origin of Internal Mammary.	Muscles of Pectoral Regions, Thyroid & Parotids
Axillary	Continuation of Subclavian to beginning of forelimb, where it becomes the Brachial, with Subscapular & External Thoracic offshoots. Leads to Radial & Ulnar arteries.	Forelimbs
Brachial Branches Brachial	From Axillary	Branches of Brachial
External or Lateral Thoracic	From Brachial near Subscapular	Pectoral & forelimb muscles

151

Subscapular	Large blood vessel near junction of Axillary & Brachial	Shoulder area
Bicarotid Trunk & Subsidiaries	From Brachiocephalic	
Common Carotid Arteries	From Bicarotid Trunk	
Left Common Carotid		(See branches of Left Common Carotid, Column 1)
Thyroid Artery	From Left Common Carotid	Thyroid Gland
External Carotid	From Common Carotid	Tongue & part of face
Internal Carotid	Branch of Common Carotid	Brain (Note: several arteries intervene which we will not track.)
Descending Aorta		
Thorax: Intercostals	Aorta from Aortic Arch to abdominal region	Ribs & body walls
Abdominal Aorta		
Coeliac	Separates to form Gastrosplenic & Gastrohepatic	Stomach, pancreas, spleen & liver
Gastrosplenic	Divides into Gastric & Splenic	
Gastric	From Gastrosplenic	Stomach
Splenic	From Gastrosplenic	Spleen
Gastrohepatic	Separates into Gastroduodenal & Hepatic	
Gastroduodenal	From Gastrohepatic	Duodenum & stomach
Hepatic	From Gastrohepatic	Liver
Anterior Mesenteric	From Aorta	Small intestine & anterior part of colon

Phrenico-abdominal	From Aorta under Kidney	Supplies lateral wall of body & diaphragm
Renal	Aorta to Kidney	Kidney
Genital	In male: Aorta to testes via Spermatic Arteries	Testes in male
	In female: Aorta to Utero-ovarian arteries	Uterus in female
Posterior Mesenteric	Aorta to Colon	Descending colon
Lumbar	Aorta (6 pairs present in Lumbar region. One pair arises from Middle Sacral region)	Muscles & skin of parts of abdominal wall
External Iliac	From Aorta ramifies to form several branches	Pelvic region & hindlimbs via branches
Circumflex Iliac	Branch of External Iliac	Abdominal wall & sides
Femoral	Branch of External Iliac	Anterior part of leg
Deep Femoral	Branch of Femoral at division of External Iliac	Thigh
Popliteal	Branch of Deep Femoral	Knee region
Saphenous	Branch of Deep Femoral	Posterior of hindlimb
Umbilical	Aorta bifurcates, forming two umbilicals; continues, & becomes Middle Sacral	To Placenta. Sends blood to Internal Iliacs
Internal Iliac	Internal Iliacs arise from Umbilicals	Pelvic area
Middle Sacral	Aorta	Sacral region
Caudal	Branch of Middle Sacral	Tail

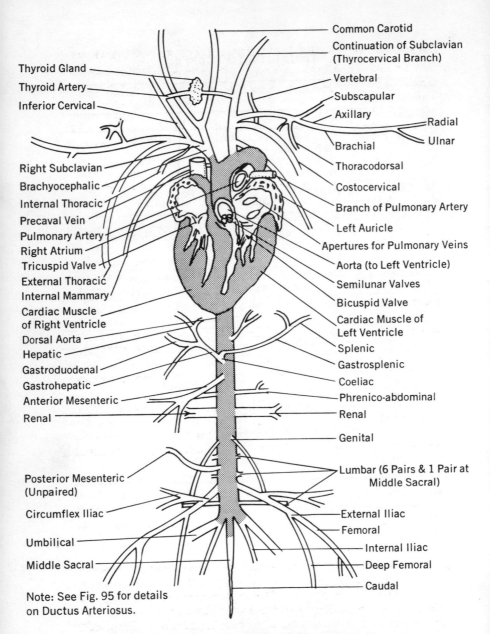

Labels (left side, top to bottom):

Thyroid Gland

Thyroid Artery

Inferior Cervical

Right Subclavian

Brachiocephalic

Internal Thoracic

Precaval Vein

Pulmonary Artery

Right Atrium

Tricuspid Valve

External Thoracic

Internal Mammary

Cardiac Muscle
of Right Ventricle

Dorsal Aorta

Hepatic

Gastroduodenal

Gastrohepatic

Anterior Mesenteric

Renal

Posterior Mesenteric
(Unpaired)

Circumflex Iliac

Umbilical

Middle Sacral

Note: See Fig. 95 for details
on Ductus Arteriosus.

Labels (right side, top to bottom):

Common Carotid

Continuation of Subclavian
(Thyrocervical Branch)

Vertebral

Subscapular

Axillary

Radial

Ulnar

Brachial

Thoracodorsal

Costocervical

Branch of Pulmonary Artery

Left Auricle

Apertures for Pulmonary Veins

Aorta (to Left Ventricle)

Semilunar Valves

Bicuspid Valve

Cardiac Muscle of
Left Ventricle

Splenic

Gastrosplenic

Coeliac

Phrenico-abdominal

Renal

Genital

Lumbar (6 Pairs & 1 Pair at
Middle Sacral)

External Iliac

Femoral

Internal Iliac

Deep Femoral

Caudal

**Fig. 93. Arterial System—Heart Hemisected From Base
to Apex Along Midsection—Dorsal Aspect Shown.**

Dissection of Heart—Some Basic Facts About the Heart

The adult heart of a mammal is a four-chambered heart with a right and left side closed off from each other by a wall or *septum*. The fetal heart differs, as pointed out earlier, because of an opening, the valved *Foramen Ovale*, between the upper right chamber, the *Right Atrium*, and the upper left chamber, the *Left Atrium*. This temporary condition is succeeded by the separateness of the right and left sides of the heart at birth.

The heart's four chambers are essentially divided into two reception and two propulsion chambers. The receiving chambers are the *left* and *right atria*, each enclosed exteriorly by a thinly muscled structure called an *Auricle*. The shape is likened to a dog's ear and therefore called "auricle," derived from the Latin word which pertains to the ear.

The propulsion chambers are the *left* and *right ventricles*, strongly powered with *cardiac muscle*, a special type of muscle tissue found in the heart. The left ventricle is more heavily muscled than the right ventricle.

Surrounding the heart is a thin membranous sac, the *Pericardium*, consisting of two layers, the *Serous Pericardium* or *Epicardium*, and the *Fibrous Sac*, with the serous layer surrounding the outside of the heart. The pericardium is a moist, slippery membrane, minimizing friction as the heart performs its contractions and relaxations.

A shallow furrow, the *Coronary Sulcus*, on the surface of the heart, appears to form a geographical boundary between the Auricles and Ventricles. Coronary vessels lie in the *Coronary Sulcus*. The upper part of the heart is called the *Base;* the lower tapered part is the *Apex*.

The fetal heart is quite small, making identification of internal structures troublesome. It would be desirable to obtain a fresh sheep or cow heart for dissection, particularly since these adult hearts are compatible with the anatomy of the human heart.

Dissection Procedures

First, the fetal heart should be freed from its vascular connections. Start by lifting the apex and locate the postcaval vein, aorta, esophagus and trachea. Use scissors to cut the blood vessels. Do not cut the esophagus and trachea. Then, moving to the base (anterior) of the heart, cut through the anterior vessels, freeing the heart. Cut through the aorta, very close to its site of emergence from the heart. Be absolutely sure to identify the ventral surface of

155

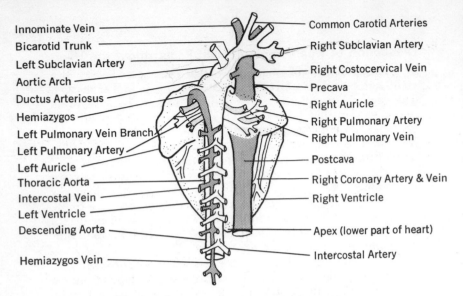

Fig. 94. Dorsal Aspect of Heart—External View.

the heart with a pin or toothpick, because in manipulating the freed heart you may temporarily become confused.

Identify all the veins and arteries associated with the anterior (base) of the heart. (See Figures 92 through 96, Table I, Part 1 and Table II, Part 1.)

Hold the heart ventral side up and raise the right auricular flap. Follow the posterior boundary of the flap as you cut laterally to the left and right, enough to enable you to lift the flap part way and examine the atrium (the interior). Note the *precaval* and *postcaval* openings. Repeat the procedure for the *left auricle* to locate the *pulmonary vessels'* connections. Direct a flexible probe through the *Foramen Ovale* between the two auricles. Examine the valves at the Foramen Ovale controlling the direction of blood flow. A magnifying lens and penlight would be helpful.

Place the heart on its left side. With a sharp scalpel gradually deepen incisions from the auricle to the apex. Separate gently as you cut, and flush the opened area with tap water. The whitish cords you see are the *tendinous cords* which anchor the *tricuspid valves,* preventing backflow of blood between the right auricle and right ventricle.

Repeat the lateral incisions on the opposite side until the cords appear, and flush this side with water. Locate the *Bicuspid Valves.* Carefully, beginning at the apex, cut left and right until

156

Fig. 95. Connections of Ductus Arteriosus—Heart Turned on Side With Left Side Facing Reader.

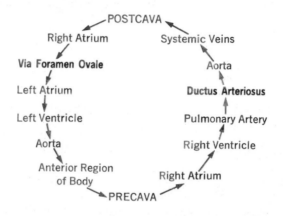

Fig. 96. Schematic of Fetal Pig Heart to Heart Circuit (Emphasis on Foramen Ovale and Ductus Arteriosus).

the ventral half of the heart begins to separate from its dorsal half. Avoid cutting the tendinous cords. Continue until the *Semilunar Valves of the Aorta* (left ventricle) and the *Semilunar Valves of the Pulmonary Artery* (right ventricle) appear. Continue separating the halves until they are freed from each other.

Note the muscular thickness of the *left ventricle*. It has to provide the major force for driving the blood through the *Systemic Circuit* which serves all of the body except the lungs. Locate the *Septum*, the wall separating the right and left halves of the heart. Find the *tricuspid* and *bicuspid valves* and with forceps open one of the flaps and try to raise it anteriorly. Observe the controlling action of the *tendinous cords* and the *Papillary Muscles* to which the cords are posteriorly attached. Identify the openings of the *pulmonary artery* and *Aorta*. Observe the *semilunar valves,* cup-shaped to prevent backflow of blood.

Give thought to the effects of inoperative valves, hardened by deposits of calcium and cholesterol, and inadequate valves, too small to close off the reverse leakage of blood. These conditions unfortunately do occur. Another pathological condition, resulting in *"blue baby"* develops when the *Ductus Arteriosus* fails to close at birth, starving the infant of its needed supply of oxygen to the tissues.

Observe that the "open" space in the ventricles seems very limited (See Figure 93, page 154). Yet, because of its remarkable muscles, responding to hormones, neural stimuli, bioelectrical stimulation and a variety of other factors, the heart is capable of an amazing output in an organism's lifespan. It is not only the quantity of output that is remarkable but the ability of the heart to respond to the moment-to-moment blood needs of the body. Run for the bus and your heart beats more rapidly. Rest, and it slows down. Its beat is always rhythmical except when diseased—a magnificent supporter of life. Protect it!

A Brief Overview of The Mammalian Brain

The nervous system is a complex coordination of cells specialized to conduct impulses throughout the organism. It enables the animal to respond to changes in its external and internal environment by receiving stimuli through *sensory nerve cells*. This serves to initiate responses of adjustment by *effectors*, generally *muscles* or *glands*. The higher forms of animal life have concentrations of *association neurons* in a special organ, the *brain*, and especially in the *cerebrum* of the brain. The presence of neuron junctions called *synapses* make it possible for the end of one neuron to transfer its impulse to one or more of several different neurons which, at their synaptic junctions, may increase greatly the potential of variety in the response to the original stimulus. The culminating effect of potential for variation in response is *intelligent behavior*. An organism that can have but one predictable behavioral response for a specific stimulus reacts by *reflex* or *instinct*. One that can produce a number of different responses to a specific stimulus performs with complex behavior to the level of intelligence.

The nervous system is an integrated complex, but for purposes of study it is considered to have two major divisions, the *Central Nervous System* and the *Peripheral Nervous System*. The former includes the *Brain* and *Spinal Cord*. The Peripheral System consists of the *cranial nerves,* the *spinal nerves' ganglia,* and organs that relate directly with the peripheral system.

The *Peripheral Nervous System* includes the *Autonomic Nervous System* which has neural control over the involuntary muscles and glands of the viscera, as well as influencing blood vessel and heart action. The *Autonomic Nervous System* is subdivided into the *Sympathetic* and *Parasympathetic Systems.* These two sub-divisions generally act antagonistically. If one tends to stimulate secretion by a gland, the other tends to inhibit secretion—a neural system of "checks and balances". The autonomic system extends from the base of the skull to the tail. *Preganglionic nerve fibers* terminate in *autonomic ganglia* from spinal nerves and certain cranial nerves. *Postganglionic fibers* begin at the ganglia and terminate at glands or involuntary muscles.

Parasympathetic fibers are connected with several cranial nerves and with the sacral section of the spinal cord and its spinal nerves. An *autonomic nerve center* is called a *plexus.*

Central Nervous System: The Brain

The brain is a highly organized concentration of nerve fiber tracts, nerve cell bodies and association neurons, protectively covered by membranes and a bony cranium and nourished by blood and cerebrospinal fluid.

Divisions of the Brain (see Figures 97 through 99, pages 162-165)

1. Prosencephalon or *forebrain* has two divisions:
   Telencephalon, front section of the brain, consists of *Cerebral Hemispheres* and *Olfactory Lobes.*
   Diencephalon, composed of nerve transmission tracts, connects the *Cerebral Hemispheres* with the *midbrain.* Its *thalamic structures* form such parts as the *Pineal Body, Posterior Lobe of the Pituitary Gland* and the *Optic Chiasma,* where fibers of the optic nerves cross over. (See Figures 97 through 99).
2. *Mesencephalon* or *midbrain* consists of the *Crura Cerebri,* tracts bridging the *Pons* and *Cerebellum* with the *forebrain.* It also has the *Corpora Quadrigemina* which are centers for sight and hearing.

3. *Myelencephalon* or *brain stem* essentially consists of the *Medulla Oblongata*, the junction of the spinal cord and the brain. It is a continuous passageway between the brain and spinal cord. The so-called "vital reflexes" such as sneezing, swallowing, breathing and so forth, are controlled by the neural components of the *Medulla Oblongata*.

Structures of the Brain

1. Cerebrum: The large convoluted mass like non-uniform corrugations is the *cerebrum*. It has two hemispheres deeply divided in its midline by a *longitudinal fissure*. Exteriorly it has indentations called *sulci* and elevations called *gyri*. The convolutions forming the outer mass of the cerebrum consist of a *gray substance* or *gray matter*. It is the *cortex* of the cerebrum. The inner mass, made up of nerve fiber tracts with white fatty sheaths is called the *white matter*. Specific areas of the cerebrum control definite functions such as sight, hearing and memory. It is the site of intelligence.

2. Olfactory Lobes: Situated at the most anterior end of the cerebrum are two large prominences, the *Olfactory Lobes*, that relate to the sense of smell.

3. Corpus Callosum: This is a central, white commissure, a band of nerve fiber tracts interlinking the cerebral hemispheres. It lies deep between the two hemispheres.

4. Cerebellum: The cerebellum is a large structure consisting of a right and left hemisphere connected by a narrow, middle bridge. It is located between the posterior, occipital portion of the cerebrum and the brain stem, the Medulla Oblongata. The *cerebellum* connects with the *Pons*, *Midbrain* and *Brain Stem*. Among other functions, it is a locus for control of balance and muscular coordination.

5. Pons: The *pons* is composed of masses of nerve fibers arching over the brain stem ventrally, like a thick band. Anteriorly, it rests against the *cerebral peduncles* of the *midbrain*. Several cranial nerves arise at the pons.

6. Corpora Quadrigemina: The *corpora quadrigemina* are four mound-like elevations called *Colliculi*, seen ventrally by spreading apart the *cerebral hemispheres* and

the *cerebellar hemispheres*. The *trochlear nerves* emerge from the corpora quadrigemina.

7. Thalamus: The *thalamus* looks like two large ovoid gray masses resting aslant, across the cephalic end of the midbrain, and on each side of the *third ventricle*. It is a synaptic "relay station" to the cerebral cortex. It controls perception of pain and extremes of heat and cold.

8. Hypothalamus: The *hypothalamus* is located at the ventral and posterior region of the *Diencephalon* at the third ventricle. It comprises the following structures:

    Mammillary Bodies: two small mounds near the *cerebral peduncles* at the midline.

    Tuber Cinereum: located between the optic chiasma and the mammillary bodies (See Figure 99, page 164). The *infundibulum*, a narrow hollow stalk, arises from the tuber cinereum and terminates ventrally in the posterior lobe of the *pituitary gland*, the *hypophysis cerebri*.

    Optic Chiasma: An "X" shaped criss-cross of nerve fibers connecting the *optic nerves* with the *lateral geniculate bodies*, near the tuber cinereum.

9. Fornix: two bands of fibers connected in the middle under the *corpus callosum* and above the *thalamus*. Its lateral legs are the *crura* which, fused above, form the *fornix*.

10. Medulla Oblongata: The caudal end of the brain, forming a transitional passage between the spinal cord and the brain. The anterior of the *medulla oblongata* is at the pons. The *central canal* of the spinal cord continues in the medulla oblongata and widens in triangular shape at its forward half, enlarging the passage into the *fourth ventricle*. (See Figures 98 and 99, pages 163 and 164). The *cortex* of the medulla is made up of *white matter*, while the inner mass of nerve cells are *gray matter*—the reverse of the cerebrum. The medulla oblongata connects with the cerebellum via extensions called the *Restiform Bodies*. It is the major center for vital reflexes.

11. Meninges: Three membranes that envelop the brain and spinal cord. The outer, relatively thick membrane is the *Dura Mater;* the middle is the *Arachnoid* and the innermost is the *Pia Mater*. The last two are very thin membranes.

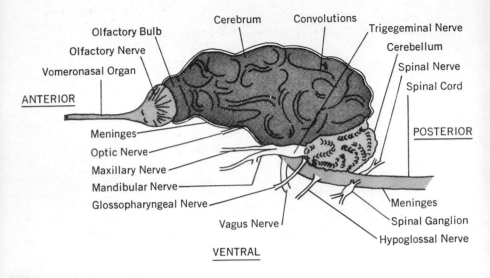

DORSAL

Olfactory Bulb

Olfactory Nerve

Vomeronasal Organ

ANTERIOR

Cerebrum   Convolutions

Trigegeminal Nerve

Cerebellum

Spinal Nerve

Spinal Cord

POSTERIOR

Meninges

Optic Nerve

Maxillary Nerve

Mandibular Nerve

Glossopharyngeal Nerve

Vagus Nerve

Meninges

Spinal Ganglion

Hypoglossal Nerve

VENTRAL

Fig. 97. External Features of Fetal Pig Brain—Left Side of Brain.

Spinal Cord (See Figures 97 and 100, pages 162 and 167)

The spinal cord is a neural "superhighway" linking the brain with all parts below the medulla oblongata. It is a slender rod solidly filled with neural tissue, except for a hollow central canal. It extends from the tail to the medulla oblongata, with which it is continuous. The cord's divisions are identical with the divisions of the vertebrae which surround it. A pair of spinal nerves emerge segmentally from the cord. Man's spinal cord has thirty-one segmental pairs. The spinal cord is covered by *meninges*. The outer mass of the cord is white matter. The inner mass, shaped grossly like a butterfly with outstretched wings, contains the gray matter. Study Figure 100 for some details of the inner structure of the spinal cord.

The dorsal part of the cord receives impulses from outside the cord and transmits them by nerve tracts to the brain or other parts, including the viscera, via the plexuses of the autonomic system. Some impulses are conducted to motor neurons located in the same spinal nerve in its ventral arm, to innervate effectors, forming a *reflex arc*. This results in a *reflex act*.

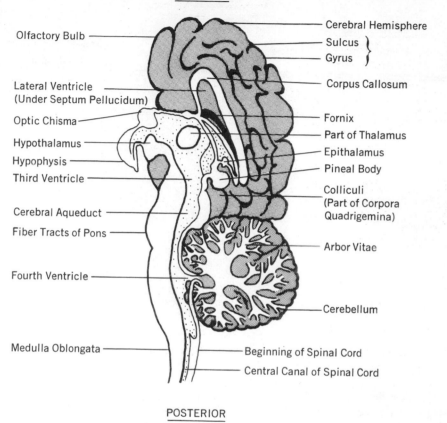

Olfactory Bulb

Cerebral Hemisphere

Sulcus }

Gyrus }

Lateral Ventricle
(Under Septum Pellucidum)

Corpus Callosum

Optic Chisma

Fornix

Hypothalamus

Part of Thalamus

Hypophysis

Epithalamus

Third Ventricle

Pineal Body

Cerebral Aqueduct

Colliculi
(Part of Corpora
Quadrigemina)

Fiber Tracts of Pons

Arbor Vitae

Fourth Ventricle

Medulla Oblongata

Cerebellum

Beginning of Spinal Cord

Central Canal of Spinal Cord

POSTERIOR

Fig. 98. Sheep Brain Hemisected—Right Side Internal Half Facing Up.

Peripheral Nervous System: Spinal and Cranial Nerves

The pairs of *spinal nerves* have *receptors* which receive stimuli at all parts of the body posterior to the brain, transmitting impulses to the spinal cord and distributing impulses through their ventral arms, to the body. Connecting with the spinal nerves are sympathetic and parasympathetic nerve centers. Such a center is a plexus. From each plexus nerves arborize to the viscera affecting the action of cardiac and smooth muscle tissue and glands.

163

ANTERIOR

CRANIAL NERVES

I | Olfactory Nerve Endings

II | Optic

III | Oculomotor

IV | Trochlear

V | Trigeminal

VI | Abducens

VII | Facial

VIII | Acoustic { Vestibular / Cochlear

IX | Glossopharyngeal

X | Vagus

XI | Spinal Accessory

XII | Hypoglossal

White Matter

Cerebrum

Olfactory Bulb

Optic Chiasma

Infundibulum

Tuber Cinereum

Mammillary Body

Cerebral Peduncle

Pons

Trapezoid Body
(Part of Central
Acoustic Pathway)

Cerebellum

Medulla Oblongata

Gray Matter of
Spinal Cord

Spinal Cord

POSTERIOR

Fig. 99. Sheep Brain—Ventral Aspect.

Cranial nerves arise from the brain. There are twelve pairs of cranial nerves, numbered sequentially in Roman numerals, generally with the first beginning at the anterior end of the brain and terminating with the medulla oblongata.

Study Table III and Figure 99, as you identify the cranial nerves.

Table III. Cranial Nerves

NO.	NAME	BRAIN CONNECTION	DISTAL CONNECTION
0.	Nervus Terminalis	Cerebral Hemispheres	Nasal Septum
I.	Olfactory	Mucus membrane of Olfactory Organ	Olfactory Lobe & Olfactory Bulb
II.	Optic	Diencephalon	Retina of Eye
III.	Oculomotor	Oculomotor nucleus of Mesencephalon	Several eye muscles
IV.	Trochlear	Medulla Oblongata: anterior part of Medullary Velum	Superior oblique muscle of eye
V.	Trigeminal	Myelencephalon-Gasserian Ganglion	Epithelium of skin, mouth & jaw muscles
VI.	Abducens	Myelencephalon	Lateral rectus muscle
VII.	Facial	Myelencephalon (See Figure 88, page 138)	Taste buds in forward part of tongue Sublingual & submaxillary glands Superficial scalp & face muscles (chin to mastoid) Platysma, muscles of ventral-lateral neck, posterior of Digastric Stylohyoid muscle
VIII.	Acoustic	Myelencephalon Vestibular Ganglion Spiral Ganglion	 Semicircular canals, utriculus & sacculus of ear Organ of Corti in ear
IX.	Glossopharyngeal	Myelencephalon	Pharynx & its muscles Parotid gland Rear of tongue
X.	Vagus	Myelencephalon	Viscera of thorax & abdomen through sympathetic ganglia Voluntary muscles of pharynx & larynx Pharynx, larynx & trachea External ear
XI.	Spinal Accessory	Myelencephalon	Voluntary muscles of pharynx & larynx Via sympathetic plexus to thoracic & abdominal viscera Dorsal anterior back muscles
XII.	Hypoglossal	Myelencephalon	Ventral neck muscles Muscles of tongue

Dissection Procedures for Nervous System

Part I. Working With the Fetal Pig

Set the specimen dorsal side up. With sharp scalpel start an incision at the midline, anterior to the eyes. Continue the incision to a midline point at the level of the anterior attachment of the ears. Cut laterally on each side, to the ears. Continue the incision anteriorly on each side but do not cut around the eyes. Complete the incision at the anterior or end to the midline.

Lift the skin and cut more deeply, following the line of initial incisions and gradually remove the skin, muscles and connective tissue until the skull is exposed. Now insert the point of the scalpel as a wedge at the edge of the posterior median cut, and begin to cut through the skull. Use forceps and scalpel to pry up pieces of the skull and break them off, until you have cleared the entire exposed dome. Then the *meninges*, the *dura mater, arachnoid* and *pia mater* membranes should be removed. Scissors will probably be most effective. At this point sever the head from the body, using your scalpel and ringing the incisions deeper and deeper until the spinal column is parted.

You will first observe the cerebrum and its hemispheres, the gyri and sulci, and the fissures (See Figures 97 and 98). Posterior to the cerebrum find the cerebellum and its hemispheres. The fetal brain is relatively small and soft and readily damaged. It is not an effective structure for dissection and study.

Examine Figure 97 and try to locate the parts listed in the illustration. Do not remove the brain from the cranial cavity because you will most likely destroy the few cranial connections that might otherwise be identifiable. Move the brain gently to the right or left to locate the cranial nerves shown in Figure 97.

Take the severed torso and place it dorsal side up on your tray. Make a midline incision all the way to the tail. Cut down to the spine. Cut away the skin and muscles about ½ inch to the right and left of the midline, exposing the spinal column. Cut away two or three vertebrae to find the spinal cord which passes through the spinal column. Find the *Filum Terminale*, a thread-like tapered end of the spinal cord. Try to trace a *plexus*, part of the *Autonomic Nervous System*, at the cervical or lumbar sections of the spinal cord. By following the path of several spinal nerves, remove the skin and muscles until you discover a network of nerves. They look like white cords. This is difficult, requiring skill and patience.

Except for studying the gross anatomy of the eye and ear, your dissection of the fetal pig is finished. For continued study of

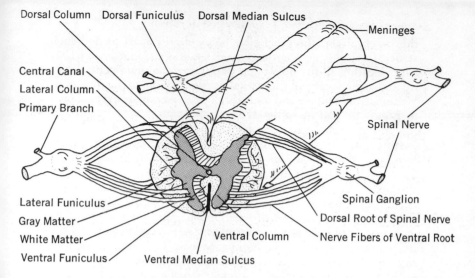

Dorsal Column   Dorsal Funiculus   Dorsal Median Sulcus

Meninges

Central Canal
Lateral Column
Primary Branch

Spinal Nerve

Lateral Funiculus
Gray Matter
White Matter
Ventral Funiculus

Ventral Column
Ventral Median Sulcus

Spinal Ganglion
Dorsal Root of Spinal Nerve
Nerve Fibers of Ventral Root

Note: "Columns" are found in Gray Matter "Funiculi" are found in White Matter
Meninges are outer covers of Spinal Cord

Fig. 100. Spinal Cord Segment.

**Schematic diagram showing segmentally
paired spinal nerves and cross section of cord
with gray matter projected.**

the Central Nervous System it is desirable to obtain a sheep brain
which is large enough, and whose texture and consistency is firm
enough for successful dissection. If sheep brain specimens are
available for examination only, not for dissection, it is possible to
identify all of the main structures apparent without cutting into
the brain itself. You should concurrently examine a dismember-
able model of a human brain or an actual human brain for purposes
of comparison and for first hand knowledge of the structure of the
human brain.

Part II. Sheep Brain

Using Figures 98 and 99 as your pictorial guide and the
description of the anatomy of the sheep brain in pages 167-168 as
your textual guide, start with an examination of the dorsal brain.
Locate the structures in Figure 98. Gently spread the cerebral
hemispheres along the deep longitudinal central fissure to find the
corpus callosum and its neighboring structures, such as the
fornix, the optic chiasma and so forth. Then proceed to spread

the cerebral and the cerebellar hemispheres apart to find such structures as the pons, corpora quadrigemina and fourth ventricle. After locating all the illustrated parts, turn the brain ventral side up and again locate all the structures discussed and diagrammed. Systematically locate and identify all twelve cranial nerves shown in Figure 99 and in Table III.

If a dissectible brain is available, make a sagittal section by cutting down dorsoventrally between the cerebral and cerebellar hemispheres until they are separated. Again, using Figures 98 and 99 as your guide, identify all the parts, continuously referring to the textual descriptions. Finally, cut a longitudinal section of the cerebrum antero-posteriorly above the level of the corpus callosum to see the interior of the cerebrum. Find the cortex and its gray matter of association neurons and nerve cell bodies and the inner mass of white matter, composed mainly of nerve tracts, with nerves encased by white myelenated (fatty) sheaths. Also cut a cerebellar hemisphere longitudinally in half to observe its internal structure of arbor vitae and nerve tracts.

Dissection of The Eye (See Figures 101 and 102, pages 169 and 170)

Carefully slit all the skin at the corner of each eye until, with forceps, you can roll back the upper eyelid. The glistening undersurface is a layer of mucous membrane continued on the eyeball, called the *conjunctiva*. At the nasal (inner) corner of each eye is a fold of the conjunctiva, the *nictitating membrane*. (See page 99, Figure 60, showing the position of the nictitating membrane in the frog). Also, at each nasal corner is the opening to the *lacrimal ducts* which receive "tears" from the *lacrimal glands*. Wash the eyes and drain the fluid through a *nasolacrimal duct*. You may be able to see the *Meibomian glands*, oil glands located on the internal surface of the eyelids. Look for thin yellow bands.

Cut along the dorsal margin of the end of the maxillary-mandibular joint, the *zygomatic arch*, removing the tissue around it to free it. Cut the lower lid at each corner down to the freed zygomatic region and peel it down, finally cutting it off. Pull the upper lid as you cut dorsally and remove it with a lateral incision. Now, using a probe, locate the eye muscle bands as you pick away surrounding tissue, gently pulling the eyeball forward until the seven eye muscles are exposed. (See Figure 101). The space in which the eye and its muscles are found is the *Orbit*. The muscles act by changing the position of the eyeball, thus enabling vision from directly forward to peripheral vision in all directions except,

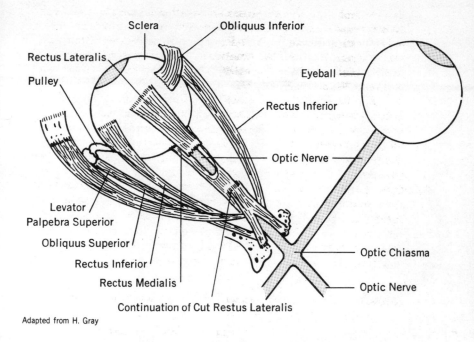

Sclera

Obliquus Inferior

Rectus Lateralis

Pulley

Eyeball

Rectus Inferior

Optic Nerve

Levator
Palpebra Superior

Obliquus Superior

Rectus Inferior

Rectus Medialis

Optic Chiasma

Optic Nerve

Continuation of Cut Restus Lateralis

Adapted from H. Gray

Fig. 101. Muscles of Eye—Schematic.

of course, backwards. Find the *optic nerve* and sever it and whatever residues of tissue continue to hold the eye in its orbit. Remove the eye. With forceps pull each muscle to get a gross idea of its effect on the eyeball.

Hold the eye in its dorso-ventral axis and cut away a circle of the outer layer, the *sclera*. (See Figure 102). The sclera encircles the eye and at its front a clear, curved elevation, the *cornea*, is present. In a preserved specimen the cornea may be cloudy. Under the cornea is the *iris*, pigmented except in albinos. The small opening in the center of the iris is the *pupil*. Under the sclera is a dark layer, the *choroid coat*, and close behind it is the *retina*, richly supplied with nerve endings that connect with the *optic nerve*. Behind the cornea is the *anterior chamber* filled with *aqueous humor*. Behind the iris is a small space, the *posterior chamber*, also filled with liquid. Extending into the posterior chamber is a relatively large *crystalline lens* which also partially

169

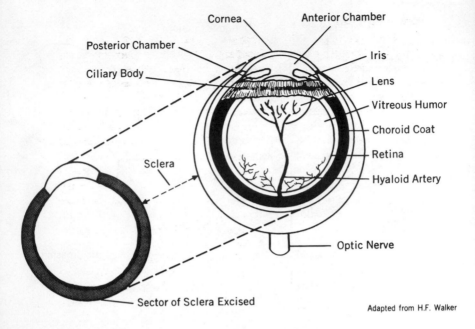

Cornea

Anterior Chamber

Posterior Chamber

Iris

Ciliary Body

Lens

Vitreous Humor

Choroid Coat

Retina

Sclera

Hyaloid Artery

Optic Nerve

Sector of Sclera Excised

Adapted from H.F. Walker

Fig. 102. Structure of Fetal Pig Eye—Shallow Cup of Sclera Removed.

occupies the large chamber that is filled with a viscous, gelatinous, transparent material. The liquid in the chamber not only keeps the eye moist but maintains a pressure tension without which the eye could collapse. A blood vessel found in the fetal eye but not in the adult eye is the *hyaloid artery*. The locus of connection between the optic nerve and the retina is the *"blind spot"*.

Remove and examine the lens. Use a penlight to flash a beam through the lens. The lens is flexible and its curvature is critical in focusing.

It is possible to dissect the ear apparatus in a fetal pig but it requires skill, since the middle ear and inner ear are very small and encased in hard tissue. A better specimen for such dissection is a preserved adult cat or rabbit.

This ends our dissection of the gross anatomy or macro-anatomy of the fetal pig. But much can still be learned about the structure of the fetal pig from your already dissected specimen.

170

Further Activities

Here are several things that should be done. Slit open a section of the digestive system structures: esophagus, stomach, small intestine and so forth. Wash and examine the internal appearance with a hand lens or a binocular microscope. Check with your biology textbook for an explanation of your findings.

Cut thin slices of muscle, liver, kidney, testis and other parts. Examine them with a binocular microscope. Refer to a book on histology to learn more about the microscopic structure of parts of the body. Compare prepared slides of cardiac (heart) muscle and involuntary muscle from the large intestine. Examine prepared slides of various glands such as the parotid, pancreas, adrenal, pituitary and so forth, always referring to histology books. Learn to prepare your own stained slides as well. Full directions are to be found in many books on microscopy and on biological techniques.

We have travelled a long way on the adventurous highway of dissection, from the relatively simple earthworm, whose body resembles a train of similar boxcars, to the complex fetal pig whose anatomy resembles that of man. On the way we discovered that every dissection unfolds a story of the past and provides us with a basis for knowing more about the animals of the present. Not only for man is it true that "All the world's a stage." Every animal plays its part in the great drama of life!

Now, it is time to discover that plants too can be dissected.

10

Flowers Can Be Dissected Too — The Gladiolus.

MOST PEOPLE think of animals when dissection is mentioned. But plants too are excellent subjects for dissection. Some of the greatest advances in science have resulted from knowledge gained through the dissection of plants. This includes advances in our knowledge of heredity, medicine, evolution, cytology, physiology and other branches of science.

A plant, like an animal, is made up of organs, tissues and fundamental units called cells. It engages in almost the same functions as an animal with two main exceptions—it does not ingest, or swallow solid food nor does it eject solid wastes. Furthermore, unlike an animal, a green plant can manufacture its own food, using the energy radiated from the sun.

Plants have had their own evolution dating back to immemorial time. In fact there was a time early in global history when it would have been well nigh impossible to distinguish between plants and animals. From these "planimals" have descended the countless strange and wonderful creatures and plants that have helped to fashion the face of the earth. Lichens and similar pioneer plants invade desolate rock, grow in the crevices and prepare living beachheads for other plants. Their remains provide a network for holding water. Animals move in, following the plants, and over long periods of time the face of the earth is literally changed by the animals and plants. From bare rock to soil to forest is a succession that has happened in many parts of the world.

Of all the parts of a plant the flower has most captivated people with its beauty of color and form. Scientifically the flower is the key to plant evolution, heredity and classification. The parts of a flower and their arrangement help us determine

MALE ORGANS–THE STAMENS:

a. Anther – produces pollen grains which develop sex cells (sperm nuclei).

b. Filament – supports anther and conducts food and water to anther.

FEMALE ORGANS–THE PISTIL:

a. Hairy stigma divided into 3 parts – holds pollen grains.

b. Style—connects stigma with ovary (pollen tube grows through style from stigma into ovary).

c. Ovary—contains ovules which develop into seeds after fertilization by the sperm nuclei of the pollen tube.

Receptacle supports ovary and conducts food to ovary.

Angle of attachment.

Step 1. To remove flower from stem cut along dotted line at angle of attachment of flower to stem.

Step 2. To reveal ovary peel down modified protective leaf (not part of flower) to lower end of ovary. Petals Nos. 1, 2, 3, (generally brightly colored) are really modified leaves.

Sepals Nos. 4, 5, 6, (small and green in most flowers) are also modified leaves.

Stem of plant.

Fig. 103. Floral Organs of the Gladiolus—A Perfect Flower.

the group to which it belongs, and help us trace its kinship with other plants. For example, botanists divide flowering plants into two groups—the *monocotyledons* and the *dicotyledons*. The dicotyledons have flowers whose parts grow in multiples of five—five *petals*, five *sepals*, etc. The monocotyledons have flowers with multiples of three—three petals, three sepals and so on. To which group would a rose, possibly growing in your own garden, with 250 petals and 5 sepals belong?

Dissection of the Gladiolus

We are going to dissect a member of the monocotyledons, the gladiolus, described in Fig. 79. The gladiolus is a complete flower with relatively large parts. It is simple to dissect and is a fine representative of one of the two great divisions of flowering plants.

Obtain a stalk or stem with several gladiolus flowers from any flower shop. You will need the instruments used in previous dissections. A microscope and a microscope slide would be helpful. Now prepare to dissect as follows:

With scalpel cut one flower from the stem as shown in Fig. 79. Identify flower parts labeled in Fig. 79.

Carefully peel down modified protective leaf until you reach lower end of ovary. Then cut the leaf off with scissors. Be careful not to damage ovary. With sharp scalpel trim remaining tissue of leaf away from lower end or base of ovary. Bend sepals backward until they crack. Cut them off at point of break with scissors. Remove the petals in the same way. Examine both surfaces of the petals and sepals with a hand lens. Observe how heavily laden they are with sap. Note that the veins show up clearly, indicating that the petal is really a modified leaf with color pigment for attracting insects.

The specimen now looks like a cup with stalks projecting outward. Let's remove each stamen and its attachment from the flower, as shown in Fig. 80a.

After you have removed the stamens, examine the *anthers* with a low power microscope or hand lens. Note the enormous number of pollen grains. Can you imagine how many pollen grains are carried from flower to flower by a single bee?

Fig. 80b shows a stamen removed from the flower. Hold the stamen at its lower end and strike the anther sharply against a glass slide. Examine the slide with a microscope under low and high power to get a better view of the remarkable pollen structures.

Ovary and Ovule of the Gladiolus

After the stamens have been removed, the only part of the specimen left to dissect is the *pistil*, the female organ of the flower. Study Fig. 80c. Examine the external appearance of the ovary with a hand lens. Note the longitudinal lines or sutures. They provide evidence of the fact that the pistil of the gladiolus is really three pistils that have fused together.

To study the inside of the ovary, we will remove a wedge from the ovary as shown in Figs. 80c and 81a. After removing wedge, examine it with a hand lens or with a low power microscope. Locate the parts labeled in Figs. 81a and 81b.

Step 1. With scalpel make 2 cuts from points A and B down to top of ovary at base of petals.

Step 2. Fold down and cut off this section of petals. Remove remaining parts of petals similarly. Do not damage the attached stamens.

Stamens (not shown),

Step 3. Examine exposed area. Note deeper streaks of color at base of petals. These act as color road maps to guide insects seeking nectar in the throat of the flower.

A
B

Style of pistil.

Ovary.

a. Removing Stamen.

b. Stamen Removed.

Anther.

Filament.

Lower end of petal.

Stigma.

Style.

c. Dissecting the Ovary.

Step 1. Hold ovary in place with forceps as shown.

Ovary.

Step 2. Make shallow cuts with scalpel down two of the division lines. Angle cuts so as to cut out wedge of ovary, as if cutting slice of cake.

Fig. 104. Removing Stamens and Dissecting Ovary of Gladiolus.

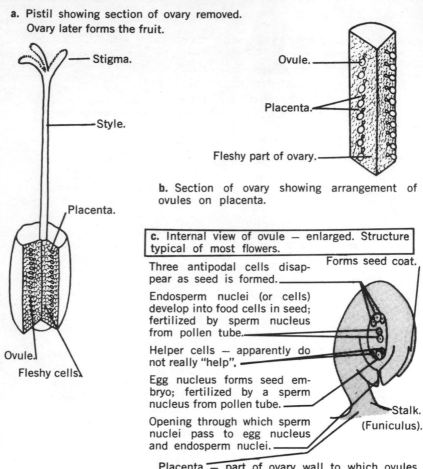

a. Pistil showing section of ovary removed. Ovary later forms the fruit.

Stigma.

Style.

Placenta.

Ovule.

Fleshy cells.

Ovule.

Placenta.

Fleshy part of ovary.

b. Section of ovary showing arrangement of ovules on placenta.

c. Internal view of ovule — enlarged. Structure typical of most flowers.

Forms seed coat.

Three antipodal cells disappear as seed is formed.

Endosperm nuclei (or cells) develop into food cells in seed; fertilized by sperm nucleus from pollen tube.

Helper cells — apparently do not really "help".

Egg nucleus forms seed embryo; fertilized by a sperm nucleus from pollen tube.

Opening through which sperm nuclei pass to egg nucleus and endosperm nuclei.

Stalk. (Funiculus).

Placenta — part of ovary wall to which ovules are attached. Contains tubes that carry food to developing seed and fruit.

Fig. 105. Internal View of Gladiolus Ovary.

The Next Generation—From Ovules to Seeds

A microscopic view of the anatomy of an ovule is shown in Fig. 81c which also describes the reproductive functions of the parts of the ovule.

Thus far we have explored the *macroscopic* anatomy (visible to unaided eye) of animals and of a flower with just a glimpse of microscopic anatomy. This opens the door to a long and exciting corridor that leads into many other fields of exploration. For example, after studying the appearance and parts of a heart with the naked eye and with a magnifying lens as we did in Chapter 8, we can go a step further. We can examine the microscopic anatomy or histology of plants and animals, or their parts. Ultimately, as a scientist, you will use the electron microscope which magnifies to about 200,000 diameters.

Project 1: Studying Microscopic Anatomy

How can you study tissues and cells of organisms? Let's take the ovary of the gladiolus as an example. Figs. 81a and 81b show the inside of an ovary, and Fig. 81c shows the inside of an ovule. To see these structures microscopically you will need a special instrument called a *microtome*. This is used to cut thin slices of the organism or of its parts. The pieces are so thin that they do not block out transmitted light as you examine them under a microscope. This transmitted light penetrates the slide and the transparent parts of the sectioned specimen. You see the opaque parts of the cells because they block out light rays and cast shadow outlines.

There are some simple, inexpensive microtomes on the market that can help you to learn a great deal about tissues. You must learn how to prepare tissues for slicing and for staining, which shows up, in color, the structures you wish to study. These techniques can be learned from a book on histology. The materials are available. The subject is fascinating. What are you waiting for?

Project 2: Science Collections in Plastic

It is now possible to preserve your plant and animal specimens by embedding or encasing them in beautiful clear plastic, shaped into any form you like. For example, you can preserve butterflies in transparent plastic shaped to form bookends, paper weights or whatever your creative mind suggests. These plastic mounts last indefinitely and remain clear as crystal. You can arrange combinations of animals and plants in these plastic molds to imitate their natural habitat or ecological setting. You can even go into business for yourself and sell beautiful gifts for Mother's Day, Father's Day and other festive occasions.

Materials and directions for using the plastic encasing

Fig. 106. Preserving Specimen by Embedding in Plastic.
Courtesy Carolina Biological Supply Company.

chemicals are sold by biological supply houses. Try this technique for pleasure and for beauty. Have fun and profit from it.

Project 3: Problems of Survival in Manned Space Ships

Man has already circumnavigated the earth in a space flight, though only for a short duration. There is enough evidence to show that he is ready to reach greater distances into space. However, keeping man alive in prolonged space flights is a horn of another dilemma. He must have a continuous supply of oxygen and means of continuously removing carbon dioxide. In addition, adequate food must be available, humidity must be controlled, temperature must be regulated, and the cosmonauts must be protected against harmful radiations. These are only a few of the difficult problems that have to be solved to insure survival in extended space flight.

All these problems have to be solved at one point, the space ship, travelling in utter loneliness and in darkness through unlivable space. Would you like to try your hand at one of the complex problems that has yet to be solved? The problem is, how to supply the cosmonaut with adequate food which, in turn, can also supply adequate oxygen and, moreover, remove from the space ship the deadly carbon dioxide man exhales—*all at the same time!* Caution: This is no cookbook project. It's wide open, and no one can predict just where it will lead. Well, let's look into the problem a little more closely.

The space ship has no room for storage of large amounts

of food and for oxygen tanks. Therefore a way must be found to have food and oxygen continuously produced within the space ship or to "hibernate" the space man so that he will have no need for food and oxygen. We will try the first alternative, which seems more practicable at the present level of knowledge.

We know that green plants can convert the sun's energy into food with the aid of water, raw materials and carbon dioxide. However, we can't plant a vegetable garden in a space ship that will do all of these things. But there is a microscopic green plant cell belonging to a group of primitive green plants known as *algae* that *can* do these things. It is called the *Chlorella vulgaris*. It grows in water which the astronauts will need, and it requires only carbon dioxide, light, temperature control and some raw materials (chemicals) which are easily supplied, to manufacture food.

Experiments have shown that the *chlorella* is an efficient food producer, rich in the nutrients needed by man. But can it be eaten by man? Yes. Chlorella has been used to make bread, soups and even ice cream. Here is one suggestion to find out whether chlorella can produce enough oxygen and remove enough carbon dioxide to keep animals alive.

Obtain two 3 or 4 gallon aquarium tanks, each with a glass top. Add about one inch of water to the bottom of each tank. Place an equal number of live frogs, from 6 to 12, in each tank. They will produce the carbon dioxide needed for the chlorella experiment. Cover each tank with its glass top. Keep the tanks in the light near a window but *not in direct sunlight*.

Prepare a culture medium for the Chlorella vulgaris. Both the Chlorella vulgaris and directions for preparing the medium may be obtained from biological supply houses. One medium used successfully is a mixture of .25 gm $MgSO_4.7H_2O$, .25 gm KH_2PO_4, .12 gm KCl, .01 cc of a 1% solution of $FeCl_3.6H_2O$ stirred in 250 ml. of water to which 1.0 gm of $Ca(NO_3)_2$ is added.

Pour this mixture into five wide-mouthed 50-100 ml bottles. Inoculate chlorella culture into each bottle with a transfer needle. (See your science teacher for explanation of transfer needle technique.) Cover each bottle with gauze. Place a drop of chlorella culture on a slide with a transfer

179

needle or a medicine dropper and, with the high power of a microscope, estimate the number of cells inoculated into each bottle. Place bottles near window for several days and make a population count daily until you see a greenish tint in the water, especially near the bottom. (Ask your science teacher to explain the population count technique.) At this point there are enough chlorella cells to produce life-sustaining oxygen.

Place the 5 bottles into one tank. The other tank will act as a control to the experiment. Smear top edges of each tank with glycerine and cover each tank with its glass cover. The glycerine will prevent leakage of air. At 3 to 4 hour intervals daily, for 2 to 3 weeks, watch the frogs' behavior in both tanks. Make respiration counts once a day. (For respiration count technique see page 118.) Tabulate the respiration counts and draw your own conclusions. Watch the control group of frogs carefully because they are likely to weaken due to the diminishing supply of oxygen in the sealed chamber. The control group has no chlorella to produce oxygen and to take up the carbon dioxide wastes produced by the frogs. When the respiration rate of the control group becomes distinctly different from that of the experimental group, remove the glass top and replace it with a piece of wire screening.

At the end of the experiment remove bottles containing chlorella from tank and make a population count.

The alert investigator will want to refine the experiment in many ways. For example, temperature of the "space ship" is an important factor in survival. You can devise methods of controlling and testing different temperature effects on the growth of chlorella, liberation of oxygen, consumption of carbon dioxide and on the respiration of the amphibian "spacemen" used in the experiment. Can you explain how this set-up imitates the conditions of a manned space ship? Does this project suggest any additional experiments which will have to be done for manned flight into outer space? Can you make your own improvements to obtain additional data from this project?

This ends our dissections projects and experiments. We hope your experiences with this book will be a first step toward the development of a lifelong interest in science and possibly toward a richly rewarding career. The door is open. Science needs you and you need science.

INDEX